HOW TO READ A FINANCIAL REPORT

HOW TO READ A

WRINGING CASH FLOW AND OTHER

Second Edition

JOHN WILEY & SONS

NEW YORK CHICHESTER BRISBANE

FINANCIAL REPORT

VITAL SIGNS OUT OF THE NUMBERS

JOHN A. TRACY CPA

TORONTO   SINGAPORE

Library of Congress Cataloging in Publication Data:

Tracy, John A.
    How to read a financial report.

    Includes index.
    1. Financial statements.   I. Title.

HF5681.B2T733   1983   657'.33   83-6591
ISBN 0-471-88859-1

Printed in the United States of America

10 9 8 7 6 5 4 3 2 1

PREFACE

I'm tempted to take all the credit for the success of the first edition. To be honest, however, I had superb editors and the publisher produced a handsome book. So my thanks go to John Wiley & Sons, and deepest appreciation to Gordon Laing and Richard Lynch. I could ask for no better editors. Also, I'm most grateful for the many favorable reviews of the first edition, from the *Chicago Tribune*, to *The Accounting Review*.

You may ask therefore: If the first edition has been such a good seller, why revise it? Recent developments in financial reporting, combined with the 1981 and 1982 changes in the income tax law, demand an updating of the book. This updating also provides the opportunity to make several improvements based on readers' comments and my experience in working with the book.

Most reviewers particularly like the centerpiece diagram in the first edition — the Master Exhibit that highlights the key connections among the basic financial statements. These cause-and-effect relationships are marked like highways on a roadmap. In this second edition the Master Exhibit has been extended to also show cash flow causes and effects. The name of the game today in business is cash flow, that's for sure.

JOHN A. TRACY

Boulder, Colorado
June 1983

PREFACE TO THE FIRST EDITION

Are you a business manager who needs a better understanding of the financial reports of your own company? Are you a banker or investor who wants better insight into the financial statements of other companies? Do you have doubts about the meaning of some items in financial reports? Are you not sure what to look for?

This book is for you.

You have an interest in financial reports, but neither the time nor the need for an in-depth knowledge of accounting. Therefore, this book contains no discussions of bookkeeping procedure, data processing, or maintaining accounting records. Just as you might explain football to a friend attending a game for the first time, this book tells you the "rules of the game" – the *basic* accounting rules – how those numbers in the financial statements were arrived at, and what they really mean.

Behind all the numbers is a simple, vital concept you must never lose sight of – *cash flow*. Business is run by keeping money moving. Financial statements report *where the money came from, where it's invested for the time being*, and, most important, *how often it has turned over*. Learning to gauge cash flow is one of the most important rewards you will get from this book.

Newspaper readers are accustomed to a quick read. Users of financial statements, in contrast, must settle for a slow read. They have to know which messages to look for, and which comparisons to make to get the messages. This book will teach you to read a financial report step by step. I've kept the number of steps to a minimum, and I make no unnecessary technical detours.

A word on accounting jargon: mastering a bit of accounting terminology is unavoidable if you want to understand financial statements. When a term is first introduced, it is carefully explained. But the way you master it is through repeated use. If at first you don't fully grasp a term, don't worry. Its meaning will become clear as we move along. By the end of the book you should have a good working knowledge of the language of accountants.

You'll look at a financial report with new awareness and new confidence in your ability to "unlock" the vital information it contains.

JOHN A. TRACY

Boulder, Colorado
October 1979

CONTENTS

HOW TO READ A FINANCIAL REPORT

1

STARTING WITH CASH FLOWS

Importance of Cash Flows:
A Cash Flow Summary for the Business

Business managers, lenders, and investors are, quite rightly, very concerned with cash flows. Cash inflows and outflows are the heartbeat of any business. So let's start here. For our example we'll use a small manufacturing business that has just completed its first year of operations. The first year of business provides a fresh start, free of carry-over problems from previous years.

A summary of the company's cash receipts and cash disbursements for the first year of business is given in Exhibit A. Exhibit A shows three sources of cash receipts and five uses (disbursements) of cash during the year. Each source and use should be fairly familiar, so the following description of the company's activities is very brief:

- The company received money from the sale of products to its customers. Also, the company borrowed money on interest-bearing notes, and stockholders invested money in the corporation.

- The company paid out money for the purchase of products sold to its customers, and also paid out money for operating expenses, as well as for interest and income tax expenses. The company bought and paid for machines, equipment items, furniture, and fixtures.

EXHIBIT A—SUMMARY OF CASH RECEIPTS AND DISBURSEMENTS DURING FIRST YEAR

CASH RECEIPTS

From customers for products sold to them	$3,726,000
From stockholders for which stock shares were issued	701,000
From borrowing on notes payable on which interest is paid	520,000
Total cash receipts for year	$4,947,000

CASH DISBURSEMENTS

For purchases of products that were sold or are being held for sale to customers	$3,294,000
For several different expenses of operating the business during the year (other than interest and income tax)	864,000
For interest on debt	43,000
For income tax on taxable income of the year	120,000
For machinery, equipment, furniture, and fixtures purchased at start of year, which will last several years	464,000
Total cash disbursements during year	$4,785,000
Increase in Cash during year (cash receipts less cash disbursements), which is the balance of Cash at year-end	$ 162,000

What Does the Summary of Cash Flows NOT Tell You?

What does Exhibit A tell you? One thing it tells you is that cash, that all-important lubricant of business activity, increased $162,000 during the year. Receipts exceeded disbursements by this amount for the entire year.

But, what does Exhibit A *not* tell you that you absolutely need to know? The two most important things that the cash summary does not tell you are:

1. The *profit* for the year.

2. The *financial condition* or position of the business at the end of the year.

Why doesn't Exhibit A tell you the profit earned during the year? Profit is the total revenue (gross proceeds) from sale of products to customers less all expenses of making the sales and operating the business. You can't count money borrowed or money invested by stockholders as sales revenue. Certainly you don't earn profit by borrowing money that has to be repaid later, or by stockholders investing capital in the business.

So the first step is to distinguish between two quite different sources of cash: (a) the cash received from sales revenue, and (b) the cash received from borrowing and stockholders' investments.

Next, we have to ask whether all the cash disbursements during the year are for expenses that should be deducted from sales revenue to determine profit. The first four disbursements in Exhibit A are certainly expense related. But the fifth disbursement is too much to charge off entirely against sales revenue for the first year. These expenditures for machines, equipment, furniture, and fixtures are *long-term* investments. These resources are used over several years. To deduct all their cost in the year of purchase would be very misleading for profit measurement.

Two Basic Types of Cash Flows

At this point, therefore, we should divide the cash flows into the two groups shown below. This division of the cash flows shows that the company raised $1,221,000 capital (from borrowing and stockholders) and invested $464,000 of the capital in certain assets, leaving $757,000 available cash.

Cash receipts from sales less cash payments for expenses cause a $595,000 decrease of cash. This "used-up" most of the available cash, leaving only a $162,000 ending cash balance. The key question here is whether the $595,000 cash decrease is the loss for the year. Has the company suffered more than a half million dollar loss in its first year? The cash decreased this amount, for sure. But are the cash flows the whole story?

(1)
Cash Flows of Raising and Investing Capital

Received from borrowing	$ 520,000
Received from stockholders	701,000
Total	$1,221,000
Spent for long-term assets	464,000
Net increase of cash	$ 757,000

(2)
Cash Flows Affecting Profit

Received from sales		$3,726,000
Spent for expenses:		
Purchases of Products	$3,294,000	
Operating Expenses	864,000	
Interest Expense	43,000	
Income Tax Expense	120,000	4,321,000
Net decrease of cash		$ 595,000

Profit Cannot Be Measured by Cash Flows

Hardly ever are cash flows during a certain period the correct amounts to measure profit (or loss) for that period. To start with, this company, like the vast majority of businesses, sells its products *on credit*. At the end of the year, this company has *receivables* from sales made to its customers during the last part of the year. These receivables will be collected (in cash) during the early part of the next year.

So the cash received during the year from customers is not total sales revenue for the year. The amount of receivables at year-end has to be added to the cash received. The *correct* sales revenue for the year is the sum of the two.

Cash disbursements are *not* the correct amounts for measuring expenses. Like sales revenue, the cash amount is not the whole story. The company paid out $3,294,000 for purchases of products during the year (see Exhibit A). At year-end, however, many products are still on hand in *inventory*. In other words, some of the products bought during the year have not yet been sold by the end of the year. Only the cost of products sold and delivered to customers during the year should be deducted as expense from sales revenue to measure profit.

Furthermore, some of its year-end inventory had not yet been paid for at year-end. The company buys its products on credit, and takes some time before paying its bills. So the company has a *liability* at year-end for these recent purchases.

The cash payments during the year for operating expenses, as well as for interest and income tax expenses, are *not* the correct amounts to deduct from sales revenue to measure profit for the year. The company also has *liabilities* at the end of the year for these expenses. The cash disbursement amounts shown in Exhibit A do not include the additional amounts of these expenses that are unpaid at the end of the year.

The main point is this: cash flows are *not* the correct amounts needed to determine profit for a period of time. Cash flows do not include the complete sales revenue and expense activities for the period. A complete accounting is necessary to measure profit.

This "complete accounting" is known as the *accrual basis*. Accrual basis accounting records the receivables from making sales on credit, and also records the liabilities for unpaid expenses, in order to determine the correct profit measure for the period.

Accrual basis accounting is also necessary to get a complete look at the company's assets other than cash, as well as its liabilities and other sources of capital.

Cash Flows Do Not Reveal Financial Condition

The cash receipts and disbursements summary for the year (Exhibit A) does not reveal the financial condition of the company. The business manager certainly needs to know the asset situation of the company, that is, how much receivables, inventory, and other assets the company has. Also, the manager needs to know the amounts of the company's liabilities. The manager has the responsibility of keeping the company in a position to pay its liabilities when they come due. And the manager has to know whether the assets are too large (or too small) relative to the sales volume of the company. Lenders and investors are also very interested in the same things.

In short, managers, lenders, and investors all need a summary report of the financial condition (assets, liabilities, etc.) of a business. And they need a correct profit performance report, which sums up sales revenue and expenses for the year. A cash flow summary is also very helpful, but in no sense does it take the place of the other two reports. The next chapter introduces these two basic accounting reports.

2

INTRODUCING THE BALANCE SHEET AND THE INCOME STATEMENT

Managers, creditors, and investors need an accounting report that summarizes the present financial condition of the business. And they need a summary report that presents the correct sales revenue and expenses for the period just ended, to know the correct profit for the period. A cash flow statement, though very useful in its own right, does not provide the information needed concerning financial condition and profit performance.

Financial condition is presented in a report called the *Balance Sheet*. The profit performance summary is called the *Income*

Statement. Both are called financial statements, or just "financials." Alternative titles for the Balance Sheet include the *Statement of Financial Condition* and the *Statement of Financial Position*. Likewise, the Income Statement may be called the *Earnings Statement* or the *Statement of Operations*. Minor variations on all these titles are common.

Exhibit B presents the Balance Sheet and Exhibit C presents the Income Statement of the same company whose cash flows are shown in Exhibit A. The form and content of the Balance

EXHIBIT B—THE BALANCE SHEET

BALANCE SHEET AT END OF YEAR

Current Assets			Current Liabilities		
Cash		$ 162,000	Accounts Payable		$ 270,000
Accounts Receivable		486,000	Accrued Expenses		117,000
Inventory		702,000	Income Tax Payable		30,000
Prepaid Expenses		90,000	Notes Payable		220,000
Total Current Assets		$1,440,000	Total Current Liabilities		$ 637,000
			Long-Term Notes Payable, at 10.0%		300,000
Property, Plant, & Equipment			**Stockholders' Equity**		
Machinery, Equipment,			Paid-In Capital (for which		
Furniture, and Fixtures	$464,000		stock shares are issued)	$701,000	
Accumulated Depreciation	116,000		Retained Earnings	150,000	
Undepreciated Cost		348,000	Total		851,000
Total Assets		$1,788,000	Total Liabilities and Stockholders' Equity		$1,788,000

Sheet and Income Statement apply to a very broad range of manufacturers, wholesalers, and retailers. In other words, these financial statements are quite typical for any business that buys or makes products that are then sold to their customers. The two accounting reports summarize the financial condition and profit making activity of a company that deals in products.

EXHIBIT C—THE INCOME STATEMENT

INCOME STATEMENT FOR YEAR

Sales Revenue		$4,212,000
Cost of Goods Sold		2,808,000
Gross Profit		$1,404,000
Operating Expenses	$936,000	
Depreciation Expense	116,000	1,052,000
Operating Earnings		$ 352,000
Interest Expense		52,000
Earnings before Tax		$ 300,000
Income Tax Expense		150,000
Net Income		$ 150,000

The financial statements you see in Exhibits B and C are for a company that has just completed its first year of business. The first year is a good place to begin the study of financial statements. For one thing, there is no carry-over from previous years. Everything you see in the financial statements has happened this year; you don't have to refer back to previous years. The complete history of the company is reported in the financial statements.

Also, all the dollar amounts reported in this company's two financial statements are fairly recent values. Thus we avoid problems caused by "old" amounts that are included in the financial statements of a company that has been in business several years. We'll get to these problems later in the book.

A business also reports a third main financial statement, in addition to its Balance Sheet and Income Statement. It's called the Statement of Changes in Financial Position. This third statement is *not* shown here — it would be a serious distraction at this point. The nature and reasons for this third statement are explained later, once we've gone through the Balance Sheet and Income Statement.

Income Statement

The Income Statement summarizes sales revenue and expenses over a period of time – for one year in Exhibit C. All the dollar amounts reported in this financial statement are cumulative totals for the period. The top line is gross proceeds, or total revenue from sales to customers. The bottom line is *net income*, which is the final profit remaining after *all* expenses are deducted from sales revenue.

The Income Statement is designed to be read in a stepdown manner, like walking down stairs. Each step down is a deduction of one or more expenses. The first step deducts the cost of goods (products) sold from the revenue from the goods sold, which gives the line called *gross profit* (sometimes called gross margin). This measure of profit is called "gross" because several other expenses are not yet deducted.

Next, operating expenses and depreciation expense are deducted, giving *operating earnings* before the interest and income tax expenses. Deducting interest expense from operating earnings gives *earnings before tax*. Subtracting income tax from this gives the final step down to *net income*.

The Income Statement shown in Exhibit C reports four profit lines – gross profit, operating earnings, earnings before tax, and, finally, net income. However, some companies report only two profit lines. They add together all expenses below the gross profit line into one total amount, which is subtracted from gross profit to go directly to net income. There's no standard rule; reporting practices differ. The four line format in Exhibit C is useful in the following discussion.

The final bottom line profit measure in the Income Statement is simply sales revenue less all expenses. Is it true and accurate? This depends on whether sales revenue is measured correctly for the period *and* whether every expense is measured correctly for the period. These basic accounting measurement rules are discussed briefly at this point:

Sales Revenue – total amount received or to be received later from customers from the sales of products and services during the period. Sales revenue is net of (excludes) the following: discounts off list prices, prompt payment discounts, sales returns, and any other allowances or deductions from the original sales prices. Sales taxes are not included in Sales Revenue, nor are excise taxes that might apply.

Cost of Goods Sold – total cost of the goods sold to customers during the period. Also, the cost of goods that were not sold but were shoplifted, stolen, or are otherwise missing, as well as write-offs and write-downs due to damage or obsolescence, are included in the Cost of Goods Sold expense for the year. So this expense usually includes an extra charge for goods that did not produce any sales revenue during the period.

Operating Expenses – broadly speaking, every expense other than Cost of Goods Sold, Depreciation, Interest, and Income Tax. *Warning:* reporting practices for these expenses are not uniform. In Exhibit C only one total expense amount is reported for all operating expenses. But, in many cases, two or more may be reported. For example, marketing expenses may be separated from administration and general expenses, which is quite proper. Even in a relatively small business, there are hundreds of different operating expenses, some rather large and some very small. They range from salaries and wages of employees (large) to legal fees (hopefully small).

Depreciation Expense – fraction of the original cost of long-term operating assets (buildings, machinery, equipment, tools, furniture, and fixtures) that is recorded to expense during this period; this is the "charge" for using the assets during the period.

Interest Expense – total amount of interest on debt (interest-bearing liabilities) for the period. Other types of financing charges may also also be included, such as loan-fees.

Income Tax Expense – total amount due the government on the taxable income earned by the business during the period. This is determined by multiplying the taxable income for the period by the appropriate tax rates, less any credits (direct deductions). The income tax expenses does not include other types of taxes, such as unemployment and social security taxes on payroll, or property taxes, which are included in Operating Expenses. However, state income taxes on the business are included.

Balance Sheet

The Balance Sheet format in Exhibit B follows fairly standardized and uniform rules of classification and ordering. (The Income Statement is somewhat more flexible.) Financial institutions, public utilities, railroads, and a few other rather specialized businesses use different Balance Sheet formats. But the large majority of industrial and retail businesses follow the Balance Sheet format shown in Exhibit B.

On the left side the Balance Sheet lists assets. On the right side it lists liabilities and owners' equity. (Sometimes assets are listed on top, and liabilities and owners' equity are on bottom.) Each separate asset, liability, and owners' equity reported in the Balance Sheet is called an *account*. Every account has a name (title) and a dollar amount, which is called its balance. For instance, from Exhibit B:

Name of Account	Amount (Balance) of Account
Inventory	$702,000

The other dollar amounts in the Balance Sheet are not accounts; they are subtotals or totals from adding (or subtracting) balances of accounts. A line is drawn to indicate that a subtotal or total is being taken.

The Balance Sheet is prepared at the close of business on the last day of the Income Statement period. If, for example, the Income Statement is for the year ending June 30, 1984, the Balance Sheet is prepared at midnight June 30, 1984. The accounts' balances reported in the Balance Sheet are the amounts at that precise moment in time. The financial situation of the business is "frozen" for one split second, as it were.

The Balance Sheet does not report the total flows into and out of the assets, liabilities, and owners' equity accounts during the period. Only the ending balance at the Balance Sheet date is reported for each account. For example, the company has an ending Cash balance of $162,000 (see Exhibit B). Can you tell the cash receipts and disbursements during the year? No, not from the Balance Sheet.

Balance Sheet accounts are subdivided into the following classes, or basic groups, in the following order of presentation:

Left Side	Right Side
(1) Current Assets	(1) Current Liabilities
(2) Property, Plant, & Equipment	(2) Long-term Liabilities
(3) Other Assets	(3) Stockholders' Equity

Current Assets are cash and those other assets that will be converted into cash during one operating cycle. Assets not directly involved in the operating cycle (such as marketable securities, or receivables from employees) are included in Current Assets if they will be converted into cash during the coming year.

The operating cycle is the basic sequence: of acquiring products – holding the products until sale – selling the products – waiting to collect the receivables from the sales – and, finally, receiving the cash from the customers. This sequence is the most basic process of a business' operations; it's repeated over and over. The operating cycle may be short, only 60 days or less, or it may be relatively long, perhaps 180 days or more.

Although not as common today, in the past the assets grouped in the category Property, Plant, & Equipment were called *Fixed Assets*. However, this term is not satisfactory. Fixed assets are not really fixed or permanent, excepting the land owned by a business. More accurately, these are long-term operating assets used by a business over several years, such as machinery and equipment, trucks, fork-lifts, office furniture, computers, and so on.

The cost of a long-lived operating asset, excepting land, is gradually charged-off over its useful life. The cumulative amount of its cost that has been charged-off since the date of acquisition up to the Balance Sheet date is in the Accumulated Depreciation account. The balance in this account is deducted from the original cost balance in the asset account.

Other Assets is a catch-all class for the those assets that don't fit in either the Current Assets or Property, Plant, & Equipment. The company in this example does not have any other assets.

The official definition of *Current Liabilities* runs 200 words, plus a long footnote. Briefly, these are short-term debts that for the most part depend on the conversion of current assets into cash for their payment. Also, other debts that will come due within one year from the Balance Sheet date are put in the Current Liabilities class. There are four accounts in this class—see Exhibit B again.

Long-Term Liabilities are debts whose maturity dates are more than one year after the Balance Sheet date. There's only one account in this class (see Exhibit B again). Either in the Balance Sheet or in a footnote to the statement, the maturity dates and other relevant provisions of all long-term liabilities should be disclosed. To simplify, no footnotes are presented here. Footnotes are discussed in Chapter 18.

Liabilities are claims on the assets of a business; cash or other assets that will be converted into cash later will be used to pay the liabilities. It's apparent, therefore, that liabilities should be accounted for in the Balance Sheet.

Liabilities are also *sources* of assets. Clearly, the total assets of a company increase when it borrows money. Also, a business has liabilities for unpaid expenses. The company has not had to use some of its assets to pay these liabilities.

The other reason for reporting liabilities in the Balance Sheet is to account for the sources of the company's assets – to answer the question: where did the company's total assets come from? A complete Balance Sheet accounting requires that all sources of the company's assets be accounted for.

In addition to liabilities, the other basic source of a company's total assets is from its owners. The *Stockholders' Equity* class reveals the rest of the sources of a company's total assets. There are two basic stockholders' equity accounts— Paid-in Capital and Retained Earnings.

When the owners (the stockholders in the case of a corporation) invest capital in the business, the Paid-In Capital account is increased. The amount of net income (profit) earned by a business less the amount distributed to its owners from the profit gives the amount of earnings retained in the business. This amount is recorded in the Retained Earnings account. The nature of Retained Earnings is confusing, and, therefore, is explained very carefully later in the book at the appropriate places.

3

PROFIT
ISN'T EVERYTHING

The Threefold Task of Managers:
Profit, Financial Condition, and Cash Flow

The Income Statement reports the profit performance of the business. The ability of managers to make sales and to control expenses, and thereby to earn profit, is measured in the Income Statement. Clearly, earning an adequate profit is the key for survival and the manager's most important imperative. But the bottom line is not the end of the manager's task.

Managers must also control the *financial condition* of the business. This means keeping the assets and liabilities within proper limits and proportions relative to each other and relative to the sales and expense levels of the company. And, managers must *prevent cash shortages* that would cause the business to default on its liabilities or to miss its payroll.

The business manager really has a *threefold task:* earning profit, controlling the company's financial condition, and preventing "cashouts." Profit performance alone does not guarantee survival. In other words, you can't manage profit without also managing the changes in financial condition caused by the sales and expenses that produce your profit. Furthermore, the profit making activity may actually put a temporary drain on cash rather than provide cash inflow.

The business manager should use the Income Statement to evaluate profit performance, and to ask a whole raft of profit oriented questions. Did sales revenue meet the goals and objectives for the period? Why did sales revenue increase compared to last period? Which expenses increased more or less than they should have? And so on. These profit management questions are absolutely essential. But the manager can't stop at the end of these questions.

Beyond the profit analysis, the business manager has to move on to *financial condition* analysis and *cash flow* analysis. In large business organizations, responsibility for financial condition and cash flow usually is separated from profit responsibility. The Vice President of Finance is responsible for financial condition and cash flow; other organization units are responsible for sales and costs. In these large companies the chief executive and the board of directors must oversee and approve the decisions of the financial vice president. But most of the details can be and usually are delegated to the financial vice president of the corporation.

In middle-size and smaller businesses, however, the top-level manager or the owner/manager is directly and totally responsible for financial condition and cash flow. There's no one else to delegate these responsibilities to.

The Trouble with
Conventional Financial Statements

Unfortunately, the typical financial statements prepared by the accountant do not "pave the way" for financial condition and cash flow analyses. Conventional financial statements are not ready made for these purposes.

The Balance Sheet and Income Statement for a business, such as shown in Exhibits B and C, do not leave a clear trail of the "cross-over effects" between these two basic financial statements. The statements are presented on the assumption that the reader understands these couplings and linkages between the two statements, and that the reader will make the appropriate connections and comparisons.

The Balance Sheet and Income Statement should be accompanied by a cash flow statement, but cash flow state-ments are not usually presented. Only recently has the rule making body of the accounting profession considered making the cash flow statement one of the *required* statements in financial reports. In the opinion of many, this change is long overdue. Managers, as well as creditors and investors, clearly need a cash flow statement that summarizes the major sources and uses of cash during the period.

Chapter 1 has already explained that cash flows are the natural center of gravity for business managers. Exhibit A (page 3) shows the cash flow summary for the company. To be most useful, however, the cash flow summary needs to be tied in with the company's Balance Sheet and Income Statement to understand the interlocking of all three statements.

EXHIBIT D—MASTER EXHIBIT
(Dollar amounts in thousands)

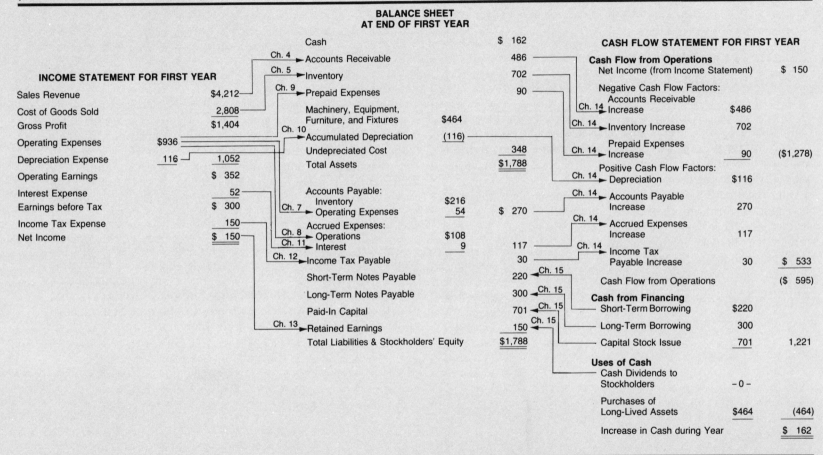

BALANCE SHEET AT END OF FIRST YEAR

Cash	$ 162
Accounts Receivable (Ch. 4)	486
Inventory (Ch. 5)	702
Prepaid Expenses (Ch. 9)	90
Machinery, Equipment, Furniture, and Fixtures	$464
Accumulated Depreciation (Ch. 10)	(116)
Undepreciated Cost	348
Total Assets	$1,788
Accounts Payable: Inventory	$216
Operating Expenses (Ch. 7)	54 → $ 270
Accrued Expenses: Operations (Ch. 8)	$108
Interest (Ch. 11)	9 → 117
Income Tax Payable (Ch. 12)	30
Short-Term Notes Payable	220 (Ch. 15)
Long-Term Notes Payable	300 (Ch. 15)
Paid-In Capital	701 (Ch. 15)
Retained Earnings (Ch. 13)	150 (Ch. 15)
Total Liabilities & Stockholders' Equity	$1,788

INCOME STATEMENT FOR FIRST YEAR

Sales Revenue	$4,212
Cost of Goods Sold	2,808
Gross Profit	$1,404
Operating Expenses	$936
Depreciation Expense	116 → 1,052
Operating Earnings	$ 352
Interest Expense	52
Earnings before Tax	$ 300
Income Tax Expense	150
Net Income	$ 150

CASH FLOW STATEMENT FOR FIRST YEAR

Cash Flow from Operations		
Net Income (from Income Statement)		$ 150
Negative Cash Flow Factors:		
Accounts Receivable Increase (Ch. 14)	$486	
Inventory Increase (Ch. 14)	702	
Prepaid Expenses Increase (Ch. 14)	90	($1,278)
Positive Cash Flow Factors:		
Depreciation (Ch. 14)	$116	
Accounts Payable Increase (Ch. 14)	270	
Accrued Expenses Increase (Ch. 14)	117	
Income Tax Payable Increase (Ch. 14)	30	$ 533
Cash Flow from Operations		($ 595)
Cash from Financing		
Short-Term Borrowing	$220	
Long-Term Borrowing	300	
Capital Stock Issue	701	1,221
Uses of Cash		
Cash Dividends to Stockholders	– 0 –	
Purchases of Long-Lived Assets	$464	(464)
Increase in Cash during Year		$ 162

A New Layout to Learn the Interlocking Nature of the Three Basic Financial Statements

Please look at Exhibit D on page 20. These are the same financial statements shown earlier, although they have been rearranged into a new layout.

First, the lines of connection between the three statements are drawn in; these serve as "tether lines" in the following discussion.

To help show these lines more clearly the Balance Sheet is positioned in the middle and it is shown in the one column (or, "report form") format—assets are on the top, and liabilities and stockholders' equity are on the bottom. The Income Statement is placed on the left and the Cash Flow Statement on the right. Near the arrow head on each line is the chapter in which the relationship is discussed.

Also notice that the format of the Cash Flow Statement is changed quite a bit from that first introduced in Chapter 1. Basically, the Cash Flow Statement now uses the bottom-line net income from the Income Statement as the starting point. This net income figure is then "adjusted" to arrive at the cash outflow (in this example) from the profit making operations of the company for the year.

In Exhibit D Accounts Payable and Accrued Expenses are divided into two parts each, to show the two separate sources of each (which are explained in later chapters). Dollar amounts are given in thousands, which is a common reporting practice by the way. A few tether lines are not drawn in (they will be made clear in later chapters), to avoid crossing over too many other lines.

So now we have all three financial statements tied together, and the important relationships among the three are made clear. Remember, these statements are for the first year of business in this example.

Financial statements are *not* reported to managers or to creditors and investors in the manner shown in Exhibit D. Accountants assume that interested readers mentally fill in the lines of connection, and make the comparisons shown in Exhibit D. Accountants probably assume too much. It takes a fair amount of understanding and some experience to know which relationships are important to look for and what these comparisons mean.

Until managers and other users develop such skills in reading financial statements, the "octopus" format shown in Exhibit D, which shows the "tentacles" of connection, is very useful. The format certainly is helpful in explaining financial statements. The Exhibit is repeated at the beginning of the following chapters, each of which focuses on one of the relationships shown in it.

Exhibit D looks rather formidable at first glance, doesn't it? Like most reports with a lot of detail, you have to take it one piece at a time, rather than in one quick sweep. It's like looking at a chess board in the middle of a game. You have to study each piece in relation to the other relevant pieces before you can see the overall pattern and situation.

We'll go carefully through each step, one at a time, in the following chapters. This will take us through Chapter 15. Then we'll quickly repeat the main points for the second year of business.

EXHIBIT D(4)

BALANCE SHEET
AT END OF FIRST YEAR

Cash		$ 162
Accounts Receivable		486
Inventory		702
Prepaid Expenses		90
Machinery, Equipment, Furniture, and Fixtures	$464	
Accumulated Depreciation	(116)	
Undepreciated Cost		348
Total Assets		$1,788
Accounts Payable:		
Inventory	$216	
Operating Expenses	54	$ 270
Accrued Expenses:		
Operations	$108	
Interest	9	117
Income Tax Payable		30
Short-Term Notes Payable		220
Long-Term Notes Payable		300
Paid-In Capital		701
Retained Earnings		150
Total Liabilities & Stockholders' Equity		$1,788

INCOME STATEMENT FOR FIRST YEAR

Sales Revenue		$4,212
Cost of Goods Sold		2,808
Gross Profit		$1,404
Operating Expenses	$936	
Depreciation Expense	116	1,052
Operating Earnings		$ 352
Interest Expense		52
Earnings before Tax		$ 300
Income Tax Expense		150
Net Income		$ 150

CASH FLOW STATEMENT FOR FIRST YEAR

Cash Flow from Operations		
Net Income (from Income Statement)		$ 150
Negative Cash Flow Factors:		
Accounts Receivable Increase	$486	
Inventory Increase	702	
Prepaid Expenses Increase	90	($1,278)
Positive Cash Flow Factors:		
Depreciation	$116	
Accounts Payable Increase	270	
Accrued Expenses Increase	117	
Income Tax Payable Increase	30	$ 533
Cash Flow from Operations		($ 595)
Cash from Financing		
Short-Term Borrowing	$220	
Long-Term Borrowing	300	
Capital Stock Issue	701	1,221
Uses of Cash		
Cash Dividends to Stockholders	– 0 –	
Purchases of Long-Lived Assets	$464	(464)
Increase in Cash during Year		$ 162

4

SALES REVENUE
↓
ACCOUNTS RECEIVABLE

Refer to Exhibit D(4). This is the Exhibit introduced in the preceding chapter, presented here again for convenient reference. Because the Exhibit will be repeated in the following chapters also, the chapter number for which the Exhibit is being used is given in parentheses.

Notice the two accounts connected in Exhibit D(4) – Sales Revenue in the Income Statement and Accounts Receivable in the Balance Sheet. The relationship between the two and the nature of each are the main topics of this chapter. You'll notice that only this one line of connection is shown in Exhibit D(4), whereas all lines of connection are shown in the "master" Exhibit D on page 20.

In this example the company made total sales of $4,212,000 during the year. When a sale is made, the amount of the sale, which basically is the price times the quantity sold, is recorded in Sales Revenue. This account accumulates all sales made during the year. At year-end, therefore, the balance in the account is the sum of all sales for the entire year.

Assume in this example that the company makes all its sales on credit. This means that cash is not received until sometime after the date of sale. The amount owed to the company, however, is immediately recorded in Accounts Receivable when each sale is made. The balance in this asset account is the amount of uncollected sales revenue.

Extending credit to customers creates a cash inflow lag. The balance of Accounts Receivable is the amount of this lag. Later, when cash is collected from customers, the Cash account is increased and Accounts Receivable is decreased.

By the end of the year most of the sales made during the year had been collected; the receivables had been converted into cash. But at year-end many sales had not yet been collected. The amount of these uncollected sales is the balance of Accounts Receivable at the end of the year.

Some of its customers pay quickly, to take advantage of prompt payment discounts offered by the company. (These discounts reduce its sales prices, but speed up its cash receipts.) On the other hand, the typical customer waits about 6 weeks to pay the company, and foregoes the prompt payment discount. The really slow customers wait 12 weeks or more to pay the company.

In sum, the company has a mixture of quick, regular, and slow paying customers; we'll assume that the average sales credit period of this company is 6 weeks. Thus, 6 weeks of the company's sales for the year are still uncollected at year-end. So the ending balance of its Accounts Receivables is computed as follows in this example:

$$\frac{6}{52} \times \begin{array}{c} \$4,212,000 \\ \text{Sales Revenue} \\ \text{for year} \end{array} = \begin{array}{c} \$486,000 \\ \text{Accounts Receivable} \end{array}$$

You'll notice in Exhibit D(4) that the ending balance of Accounts Receivable is indeed $486,000.

The main point here is that the average sales credit period determines the size of Accounts Receivable relative to annual sales revenue. The longer the average sales credit period, the larger the Accounts Receivable.

Let's approach this key point from another direction. Using information in the financial statements, we can determine the average sales credit period. The first step is to compute the following ratio:

$$\frac{\$4,212,000 \text{ Sales Revenue for year}}{\$486,000 \text{ Accounts Receivable}} = 8.67$$

This computation gives the *accounts receivable turnover ratio*. This number divided into 52 weeks gives the average sales credit period expressed in number of weeks:

$$\frac{52 \text{ weeks}}{8.67 \text{ Accounts Receivable turnover ratio}} = 6 \text{ weeks}$$

Time is the essence of the matter here. What interests the manager, and the company's creditors and investors as well, is how long it takes on average to turn its receivables into cash. The accounts receivable turnover ratio is most meaningful when it is used to determine the number of weeks (or days) it takes the company to convert its receivables into cash.

You may argue that 6 weeks is too long an average sales credit period for the company. This is precisely the point: what should it be? The manager in charge has to decide whether the average sales credit period is getting out of hand. The manager can shorten credit terms, shut off credit to slow payers, or step up collection efforts.

This is not the place to discuss customer credit policies relative to selling strategies and customer relations, which would take us far into the fields of marketing, and credits and collections. But to make an important point here: assume that without losing any sales the company's average sales credit period had been only 5 weeks, instead of the 6 weeks assumed in the financial statements of the company. In this case the ending balance of Accounts Receivable would have been $81,000 less, which is the average sales revenue per week ($4,212,000 ÷ 52 weeks = $81,000). The company would have collected $81,000 more cash during the year.

With such additional cash inflow the company could have borrowed $81,000 less. At a 10% annual interest rate this would have saved $8,100 interest expense before income tax. Or the owners could have invested $81,000 less in the business and put their money elsewhere. The point is, of course, that capital has a high cost. Excess Accounts Receivable means that excess debt, or excess owners' equity capital, is being used by the business.

A slow-up in collecting customers' receivables, or a deliberate shift in company policy allowing longer credit terms, would cause Accounts Receivable to increase. Additional capital would have to be secured, or the company would have to try and get by on a smaller cash balance.

If you were the manager in this example you would have to decide whether the size of Accounts Receivable, being 6 weeks of annual sales revenue, is consistent with the company's sales credit terms and collection policies. Perhaps 6 weeks is too long and you need to take action. If you were a creditor or an investor, you should be very interested in whether the manager is allowing the average sales credit period to get out of control. And you should be interested in any major change in the average sales credit period that may signal a major change in the company's policies.

EXHIBIT D (5)

INCOME STATEMENT FOR FIRST YEAR

Sales Revenue		$4,212
Cost of Goods Sold		2,808
Gross Profit		$1,404
Operating Expenses	$936	
Depreciation Expense	116	1,052
Operating Earnings		$ 352
Interest Expense		52
Earnings before Tax		$ 300
Income Tax Expense		150
Net Income		$ 150

BALANCE SHEET
AT END OF FIRST YEAR

Cash		$ 162
Accounts Receivable		486
Inventory		702
Prepaid Expenses		90
Machinery, Equipment, Furniture, and Fixtures	$464	
Accumulated Depreciation	(116)	
Undepreciated Cost		348
Total Assets		$1,788
Accounts Payable:		
Inventory	$216	
Operating Expenses	54	$ 270
Accrued Expenses:		
Operations	$108	
Interest	9	117
Income Tax Payable		30
Short-Term Notes Payable		220
Long-Term Notes Payable		300
Paid-In Capital		701
Retained Earnings		150
Total Liabilities & Stockholders' Equity		$1,788

CASH FLOW STATEMENT FOR FIRST YEAR

Cash Flow from Operations		
Net Income (from Income Statement)		$ 150
Negative Cash Flow Factors:		
Accounts Receivable Increase	$486	
Inventory Increase	702	
Prepaid Expenses Increase	90	($1,278)
Positive Cash Flow Factors:		
Depreciation	$116	
Accounts Payable Increase	270	
Accrued Expenses Increase	117	
Income Tax Payable Increase	30	$ 533
Cash Flow from Operations		($ 595)
Cash from Financing		
Short-Term Borrowing	$220	
Long-Term Borrowing	300	
Capital Stock Issue	701	1,221
Uses of Cash		
Cash Dividends to Stockholders	– 0 –	
Purchases of Long-Lived Assets	$464	(464)
Increase in Cash during Year		$ 162

5

COST OF GOODS SOLD

INVENTORY

To begin, refer to Exhibit D(5). Notice the two accounts connected—Cost of Goods Sold in the Income Statement and Inventory in the Balance Sheet. The relationship between these two accounts and the nature of each are the topics of this chapter.

Cost of Goods Sold is, by far, the largest expense in the Income Statement. It's deducted from Sales Revenue to determine *gross profit*, which is the first of the four profit lines reported in the Income Statement.

Gross profit is called gross because no other expenses have been deducted. Only the cost of buying (or making) the product is deducted from sales revenue at this point. Gross profit is the starting point for earning an adequate final profit (net income). In other words, the first step is to sell the products (goods) for enough gross profit, so that all the other expenses of the business can be covered. These other expenses are discussed in later chapters.

In this example the company earned a gross profit equal to 33⅓% of its sales revenue:

$$\frac{\$1,404,000 \text{ gross profit}}{\$4,212,000 \text{ sales revenue}} = 33\tfrac{1}{3}\%$$

The company sells a mix of different products, not all at the same gross profit margin (percent of sales price). In total, for all products sold during the year, its average gross profit is 33⅓%, which is fairly typical for a broad cross section of businesses.

To sell products a business must carry a stock of products, on hand and ready for delivery to its customers. This stock of products, the goods being held for sale, is called *Inventory*. So making sales causes Inventory to appear in the Balance Sheet. The line of connection is not with Sales Revenue, but rather with Cost of Goods Sold, because Inventory is reported at cost in the Balance Sheet, *not* at its sales value.

When a company buys products, its Inventory account is increased by the cost of the goods. This cost is kept in the Inventory asset account until the items are sold and delivered to customers when making sales. At this time the cost is removed from the asset and charged to Cost of Goods Sold expense. (If products become definitely unsalable or are stolen, their cost is removed from Inventory and charged to expense.)

The Inventory balance at year-end—$702,000 in this example, as shown in Exhibit D(5)—is the cost of products awaiting sale next year. The $2,808,000 deducted from Sales Revenue in the Income Statement is the cost of the goods that were sold during the year; of course, none of these products are on hand in Inventory at year-end.

Some of the company's products may come in and go out in a week or two; other goods may stay in stock 4 months or longer. As usual, holding periods differ for different products. The company's average inventory holding period, given the mix of all its products, is assumed to be 13 weeks in this example.

In other words, the quantity of goods in inventory is enough for 13 weeks of average sales. As just mentioned, inventory is recorded at cost. So 13 weeks of sales here means 13 weeks of cost of goods sold, not 13 weeks of sales revenue. Knowing that the average inventory holding period is 13 weeks, the company's Inventory balance is computed as follows in this example:

$$\frac{13}{52} \times \underset{\text{Cost of Goods Sold for year}}{\$2,808,000} = \underset{\text{Inventory}}{\$702,000}$$

You'll notice in Exhibit D(5) that the ending balance of Inventory is indeed $702,000.

The main point is that the average inventory holding period determines the size of Inventory relative to annual cost of goods sold. The longer the holding period, the larger the Inventory.

Let's approach this key point from another direction. Using information available from the financial statements, we can determine the average inventory holding period. The first step is to compute the following ratio:

$$\frac{\$2,808,000 \text{ Cost of Goods Sold for year}}{\$702,000 \text{ Inventory}} = 4.00$$

This gives the *inventory turnover ratio*. This number divided into 52 weeks gives the average inventory holding period expressed in number of weeks:

$$\frac{52 \text{ weeks}}{4.00 \text{ Inventory turnover ratio}} = 13 \text{ weeks}$$

Time is the essence of the matter here, as it is with the average sales credit period discussed in the preceding chapter. What interests the manager, and the company's creditors and investors as well, is how long the company holds an average item of inventory before it's sold. The inventory turnover ratio is most meaningful when it is used to determine the number of weeks (or days) it takes the company before the inventory is sold.

Is 13 weeks too long? Should the company's average inventory holding period be shorter? This is precisely the key question that business managers, creditors, and investors should be concerned with. If the holding period is longer than really necessary, too much capital is being tied up in inventory, and, as already mentioned, capital has a high cost. Or the company may be cash poor because it has too much money in inventory and not enough in the bank.

If the company could reduce its inventory holding period to, say, 11 weeks, $108,000 capital would be saved ($54,000 cost of goods sold per week × 2 weeks less inventory = $108,000 less capital required). However, with only 11 weeks average inventory, the company may be unable to make many sales because certain products were not available when needed. In other words, if the average inventory holding period is too low, the result may be stock-outs of certain goods, or not being able to get the goods as soon as needed to make sales. The cost of carrying inventory has to be balanced against the profit opportunities lost by not having the products in stock ready for sale.

In short, managers, and creditors and investors as well, should be concerned that the average inventory holding period is neither too high nor too low. If too high, capital is being wasted; if too low, profit opportunities are being missed. Comparisons with other companies in the same line of business and historical trends provide the guidelines for testing a company's inventory holding period.

EXHIBIT D(6)

BALANCE SHEET
AT END OF FIRST YEAR

Cash	$ 162
Accounts Receivable	486
Inventory	702
Prepaid Expenses	90

INCOME STATEMENT FOR FIRST YEAR

Sales Revenue		$4,212
Cost of Goods Sold		2,808
Gross Profit		$1,404
Operating Expenses	$936	
Depreciation Expense	116	1,052
Operating Earnings		$ 352
Interest Expense		52
Earnings before Tax		$ 300
Income Tax Expense		150
Net Income		$ 150

Machinery, Equipment, Furniture, and Fixtures	$464	
Accumulated Depreciation	(116)	
Undepreciated Cost		348
Total Assets		$1,788
Accounts Payable:		
Inventory	$216	
Operating Expenses	54	$ 270
Accrued Expenses:		
Operations	$108	
Interest	9	117
Income Tax Payable		30
Short-Term Notes Payable		220
Long-Term Notes Payable		300
Paid-In Capital		701
Retained Earnings		150
Total Liabilities & Stockholders' Equity		$1,788

CASH FLOW STATEMENT FOR FIRST YEAR

Cash Flow from Operations		
Net Income (from Income Statement)		$ 150
Negative Cash Flow Factors:		
Accounts Receivable Increase	$486	
Inventory Increase	702	
Prepaid Expenses Increase	90	($1,278)
Positive Cash Flow Factors:		
Depreciation	$116	
Accounts Payable Increase	270	
Accrued Expenses Increase	117	
Income Tax Payable Increase	30	$ 533
Cash Flow from Operations		($ 595)
Cash from Financing		
Short-Term Borrowing	$220	
Long-Term Borrowing	300	
Capital Stock Issue	701	1,221
Uses of Cash		
Cash Dividends to Stockholders	– 0 –	
Purchases of Long-Lived Assets	$464	(464)
Increase in Cash during Year		$ 162

6

INVENTORY
↓
ACCOUNTS PAYABLE

Please note in Exhibit D(6) the line linking Inventory with Accounts Payable in the Balance Sheet, which also passes through Cost of Goods Sold in the Income Statement.

To set the stage here, let's review very briefly the last two chapters. The sales prices of goods (products) sold are accumulated in the Sales Revenue account. Sales made on credit cause Accounts Receivable; the longer the credit period, the larger the Accounts Receivable. The cost of goods sold is accumulated in the Cost of Goods Sold expense account. Products must be bought and held in Inventory before they are sold. The longer the holding period, the larger the Inventory.

Inventory is closely related to Cost of Goods Sold; it's also closely related to Accounts Payable. This second relationship is the main topic of this chapter.

Businesses purchase their inventory on credit. COD (cash on delivery) purchase terms are not often encountered, unless a company is in financial trouble or has a lousy credit rating. So the typical business does not make immediate payment for its inventory purchases. (Manufacturers also buy their raw materials and production supplies on credit; the main points in the following discussion apply to these types of items as well.)

When inventory is purchased on credit, the liability for the amount of goods bought is recorded in Accounts Payable. As mentioned in the preceding chapter, the cost is also recorded in Inventory; both the asset and the liability increase the same amount.

Some purchases are paid quickly, to take advantage of prompt payment discounts offered by suppliers. But many bills are not paid until 2 months or so after purchase. Based on its payments experience and policies, a business can determine the average credit period it waits before paying for its inventory purchases. In this example, we'll assume that the average inventory purchases credit period is 4 weeks.

In other words, from the date of purchase to the date of payment is 4 weeks on average. So the last 4 weeks of inventory purchases had not been paid yet at year-end. Purchases may vary week to week; in this example, however, we assume that after the initial inventory build-up early in the year, purchases since then have been fairly equal week to week to replace goods sold and keep inventory at a stable level.

The average cost of goods sold per week (equal to purchases per week here) is $54,000 ($2,808,000 cost of goods sold per year ÷ 52 weeks = $54,000). So the Accounts Payable amount from inventory purchases is computed as follows in this example:

$54,000	×	4 weeks inventory	=	$216,000
Cost of Goods Sold (and purchases) per week		purchase credit period		Accounts Payable

See this connection in Exhibit D(6).

Sometimes at year-end the amount of Accounts Payable from inventory purchases may be higher than normal. The company may have made a large purchase just before year-end because of a supply shortage forecast or in anticipation of price increases. Or, the company may have deliberately slowed down payment of its bills towards year-end to conserve its cash balance, which would cause a temporary bulge in Accounts Payable.

BALANCE SHEET
AT END OF FIRST YEAR

Cash	$ 162
Accounts Receivable	486
Inventory	702
Prepaid Expenses	90
Machinery, Equipment, Furniture, and Fixtures	$464
Accumulated Depreciation	(116)
Undepreciated Cost	348
Total Assets	$1,788

Accounts Payable:		
Inventory	$216	
Operating Expenses	54	$ 270
Accrued Expenses:		
Operations	$108	
Interest	9	117
Income Tax Payable		30
Short-Term Notes Payable		220
Long-Term Notes Payable		300
Paid-In Capital		701
Retained Earnings		150
Total Liabilities & Stockholders' Equity		$1,788

INCOME STATEMENT FOR FIRST YEAR

Sales Revenue		$4,212
Cost of Goods Sold		2,808
Gross Profit		$1,404
Operating Expenses	$936	
Depreciation Expense	116	1,052
Operating Earnings		$ 352
Interest Expense		52
Earnings before Tax		$ 300
Income Tax Expense		150
Net Income		$ 150

CASH FLOW STATEMENT FOR FIRST YEAR

Cash Flow from Operations

Net Income (from Income Statement)		$ 150
Negative Cash Flow Factors:		
Accounts Receivable Increase	$486	
Inventory Increase	702	
Prepaid Expenses Increase	90	($1,278)
Positive Cash Flow Factors:		
Depreciation	$116	
Accounts Payable Increase	270	
Accrued Expenses Increase	117	
Income Tax Payable Increase	30	$ 533
Cash Flow from Operations		($ 595)

Cash from Financing

Short-Term Borrowing	$220	
Long-Term Borrowing	300	
Capital Stock Issue	701	1,221

Uses of Cash

Cash Dividends to Stockholders		-0-
Purchases of Long-Lived Assets	$464	(464)
Increase in Cash during Year		$ 162

7

OPERATING EXPENSES
↓
ACCOUNTS PAYABLE

Have you looked at Exhibit D(7)? Note the linkage between Operating Expenses in the Income Statement and Accounts Payable in the Balance Sheet. This relationship and the nature of these two accounts are discussed in this chapter.

Operating Expenses is a conglomerate account in the Income Statement, which includes all the different expenses of running the business *except* Depreciation Expense. The Depreciation Expense is unique and is reported separate from the Operating Expenses. Depreciation is discussed in Chapter 10.

Included under the umbrella of Operating Expenses are the following (in no particular order):

- Rent of land and buildings (in this example the company leases the land and the buildings it uses)
- Wages and salaries paid officers, office employees, salespersons, warehouse workers, and so on
- Payroll taxes and other fringe benefit costs of labor
- Office and data processing supplies, and machine rentals
- Property taxes
- Telephone
- Utilities (water, gas, electricity)
- General liability insurance, and fire insurance on contents, buildings, and property owned by the business
- Advertising and sales promotion costs
- Bad debts (which are credit sales never collected)

Many other specific operating expenses could be listed.

One reason for grouping all operating expenses (except depreciation) into one total account in the Income Statement is that the basic accounting for all these expenses can be explained in the same way. This chapter explains how operating expenses affect Accounts Payable. The next two chapters explain how operating expenses also affect two other Balance Sheet accounts.

It would be simple if every dollar of operating expenses charged to the year also were a dollar actually paid out in that same year. It would be nice and easy to equate operating expenses with cash disbursements; no other Balance Sheet (except Cash) would be affected by these expenses. But it's not quite that simple. Many operating expenses must be recorded *before* they are paid.

For example, on December 27 the company receives a bill from the utility company for power usage during the month period ending December 20. (Assume the company's accounting year ends December 31.) The amount of this expense clearly belongs in this year, so it is recorded in Accounts Payable.

This is just one example of many such unpaid operating expenses at the end of a company's accounting year. Other examples are bills from lawyers and CPAs for services, bills from newspapers for advertisements already run in the papers, telephone bills, and so on. Generally speaking, the credit terms of these payables are not long, 1 to 4 weeks being typical.

In this example we'll assume that the average credit period of the company's payables from unpaid operating expenses is 3 weeks. So, 3 weeks of its total operating expenses for the year are in Accounts Payable at year-end. In this example the average amount of operating expenses per week is $18,000

($936,000 operating expenses for year ÷ 52 weeks = $18,000). The amount of Accounts Payable at year-end from operating expenses is computed as follows:

$18,000   × 3 weeks average = $54,000
Operating Expenses   credit period   Accounts Payable
per week

See in Exhibit D(7) that this amount is included in Accounts Payable.

Recall that inventory purchases on credit are also recorded in Accounts Payable. This liability account thus has a total balance of $270,000 at year-end ($216,000 from inventory purchases + $54,000 from operating expenses).

Every bill (or invoice) for goods or services received by the business is recorded in Accounts Payable. The immediate recording of these bills is necessary to recognize the liability, and to recognize the increase of inventory or the increase of operating expense. However, the recording of these payables does *not* decrease Cash; there is no cash outflow. This very important point is discussed in Chapter 14, which deals with the cash flow analysis of net income.

INCOME STATEMENT FOR FIRST YEAR

Sales Revenue		$4,212
Cost of Goods Sold		2,808
Gross Profit		$1,404
Operating Expenses	$936	
Depreciation Expense	116	1,052
Operating Earnings		$ 352
Interest Expense		52
Earnings before Tax		$ 300
Income Tax Expense		150
Net Income		$ 150

**BALANCE SHEET
AT END OF FIRST YEAR**

Cash		$ 162
Accounts Receivable		486
Inventory		702
Prepaid Expenses		90
Machinery, Equipment, Furniture, and Fixtures	$464	
Accumulated Depreciation	(116)	
Undepreciated Cost		348
Total Assets		$1,788
Accounts Payable:		
Inventory	$216	
Operating Expenses	54	$ 270
Accrued Expenses:		
Operations	$108	
Interest	9	117
Income Tax Payable		30
Short-Term Notes Payable		220
Long-Term Notes Payable		300
Paid-In Capital		701
Retained Earnings		150
Total Liabilities & Stockholders' Equity		$1,788

CASH FLOW STATEMENT FOR FIRST YEAR

Cash Flow from Operations		
Net Income (from Income Statement)		$ 150
Negative Cash Flow Factors:		
Accounts Receivable Increase	$486	
Inventory Increase	702	
Prepaid Expenses Increase	90	($1,278)
Positive Cash Flow Factors:		
Depreciation	$116	
Accounts Payable Increase	270	
Accrued Expenses Increase	117	
Income Tax Payable Increase	30	$ 533
Cash Flow from Operations		($ 595)
Cash from Financing		
Short-Term Borrowing	$220	
Long-Term Borrowing	300	
Capital Stock Issue	701	1,221
Uses of Cash		
Cash Dividends to Stockholders	– 0 –	
Purchases of Long-Lived Assets	$464	(464)
Increase in Cash during Year		$ 162

8

OPERATING EXPENSES
↓
ACCRUED EXPENSES (PAYABLE)

Refer to the connection in Exhibit D(8) linking Operating Expenses in the Income Statement with Accrued Expenses in the Balance Sheet.

Now let's return to the utility expense example discussed in Chapter 7. Clearly, the utility cost through December 20 should be recorded in expense for the year. The utilities have been used in the operations of the business, and an actual bill has been received that is a clear and definite liability of the business. Now what about the utility usage from December 20 through December 31? The cost of utility usage for this last third of the month has not yet been billed to the business, nor even measured by the utility company, for that matter.

The accountant estimates the amount of this expense for the last third of December, and records this amount so that total operating expenses include the full amount for the entire year. However, by December 31 no bill had been received from the utility company. The company had a liability for sure – an *unbilled* liability. So a different type of liability is recorded, called *Accrued Expenses*.

The Accrued Expenses liability is separated from Accounts Payable for two reasons. First, the amounts recorded in the Accrued Expenses liability are *estimates*, which depend on the methods and reliability of the methods used to make the estimates. In contrast, the amounts recorded in Accounts Payable are definite amounts. Second, the Accounts Payable are actual bills (invoices) in the hands of the company; Accrued Expenses are liabilities for which no bills have been received.

What are some of the estimated liabilities recorded in Accrued Expenses? More than you probably would guess. In addition to the utility expense example discussed above, the Accrued Expenses liability usually includes the following:

- Accumulated vacation and sick leave pay earned by employees, which has not yet been paid by the company; this can add up to a sizable amount

- Unpaid sales commissions earned by the company's salespersons that will be paid later

- Portions of annual property taxes that should be charged to this year that haven't been billed to the company yet

- Partial-month telephone costs that have been incurred but not yet billed to the company at year-end

In summary, about a third-month of utility cost, perhaps a half-month of telephone cost, maybe a half-year of employees' vacation cost, and several other such accumulated expenses had been recorded in the Accrued Expenses at the end of the year. Not recording these liabilities would have caused a serious error in the profit measure for the year. Moreover, these are real liabilities, even though the amounts are estimated and no bills have been received.

In this example the average time before paying these liabilities is assumed to be 6 weeks. In other words, 6 weeks of its annual operating expenses are in Accrued Expenses at year-end. As computed in Chapter 7, the average operating expenses per week is $18,000 (see page 37). So the amount of Accrued Expenses from operating expenses is computed as follows:

$18,000 Operating Expenses per week	×	6 weeks average credit period	=	$108,000 Accrued Expenses

See in Exhibit D(8) that the Accrued Expenses balance includes this amount.

The Accrued Expenses amount relative to total annual operating expenses may be more or less than 6 weeks for another business. Experience provides the guideline for each individual business. For many businesses 6 weeks is about right, even though this ratio may look rather high, especially if we consider both the Accrued Expenses (estimated unbilled liabilities) and Accounts Payable (definite billed liabilities). In Chapter 7 we see that 3 weeks of our company's total annual operating expenses are in Accounts Payable at year-end, and in this chapter we see that 6 weeks are in Accrued Expenses at year-end.

In summary, 9 weeks of the company's total operating expenses for the year are unpaid at year-end, which relieved the company of having to come up with this much cash for operating expenses during the year. The company avoided $162,000 of cash pay-out during the year ($54,000 Accounts Payable plus $108,000 Accrued Expenses).

If the company could have stretched the average wait (or credit period) for paying its operating expenses from 9 weeks to, say, 11 weeks, it could have avoided an additional $36,000 of cash disbursements ($18,000 average operating expenses per week × 2 additional weeks of waiting to pay the expenses = $36,000). So the Accounts Payable and Accrued Expenses resulting from operating expenses have a significant impact on cash flow. Any change in the size of these two liabilities relative to annual operating expenses has a cash flow impact that should not be ignored by the company's managers, as well as the creditors and investors who use its financial statements.

In Exhibit D(8) you probably have noticed that there is another, though much smaller, source of Accrued Expenses – that is, the unpaid interest expense at year-end. This is discussed in Chapter 11.

Accrued Expenses and Accounts Payable result from the normal delay in paying for operating expenses. The expense is recorded now but paid for later; the liability bridges the two dates. In contrast, some expenses are paid for now but not recorded as an expense (deduction against sales revenue) until later. This reverse situation is discussed in the next chapter.

BALANCE SHEET
AT END OF FIRST YEAR

Cash		$ 162
Accounts Receivable		486
Inventory		702
▶ Prepaid Expenses		90
Machinery, Equipment, Furniture, and Fixtures	$464	
Accumulated Depreciation	(116)	
Undepreciated Cost		348
Total Assets		$1,788
Accounts Payable:		
Inventory	$216	
Operating Expenses	54	$ 270
Accrued Expenses:		
Operations	$108	
Interest	9	117
Income Tax Payable		30
Short-Term Notes Payable		220
Long-Term Notes Payable		300
Paid-In Capital		701
Retained Earnings		150
Total Liabilities & Stockholders' Equity		$1,788

INCOME STATEMENT FOR FIRST YEAR

Sales Revenue		$4,212
Cost of Goods Sold		2,808
Gross Profit		$1,404
Operating Expenses	$936 ◀	
Depreciation Expense	116	1,052
Operating Earnings		$ 352
Interest Expense		52
Earnings before Tax		$ 300
Income Tax Expense		150
Net Income		$ 150

CASH FLOW STATEMENT FOR FIRST YEAR

Cash Flow from Operations		
Net Income (from Income Statement)		$ 150
Negative Cash Flow Factors:		
Accounts Receivable Increase	$486	
Inventory Increase	702	
Prepaid Expenses Increase	90	($1,278)
Positive Cash Flow Factors:		
Depreciation	$116	
Accounts Payable Increase	270	
Accrued Expenses Increase	117	
Income Tax Payable Increase	30	$ 533
Cash Flow from Operations		($ 595)
Cash from Financing		
Short-Term Borrowing	$220	
Long-Term Borrowing	300	
Capital Stock Issue	701	1,221
Uses of Cash		
Cash Dividends to Stockholders	– 0 –	
Purchases of Long-Lived Assets	$464	(464)
Increase in Cash during Year		$ 162

9

OPERATING EXPENSES

PREPAID EXPENSES

To begin, refer to the connection in Exhibit D(9) linking Operating Expenses in the Income Statement with Prepaid Expenses in the Balance Sheet. The title of the chapter means that certain operating expenses cause Prepaid Expenses to appear in the Balance Sheet. However, the actual sequence of events is that certain operating costs are first paid in advance (prepaid), and then not until later are they charged off to expense.

Several operating costs must be paid for *before* these costs should be recorded as expense. There is a cash outlay before the amount should be recorded as an expense (as a deduction against sales revenue to measure profit for the period). For example, insurance premiums must be paid in advance of the insurance policy period. Office supplies are bought in quantities that last 2 or 3 months. Annual property taxes frequently are paid at the start of the tax assessment year. There are many more such examples of what are called *prepaid expenses*.

When paid, the cost is initially recorded in Prepaid Expenses, which is an asset account. The amount is allocated so that each future month receives its "fair share" of the cost. Each month the appropriate part of the cost is taken out of Prepaid Expenses and recorded in expense. All of the costs initially recorded in Prepaid Expenses are later taken out and put in expense in the correct months.

Based on its experience and operations, a company can determine how large, on average, its Prepaid Expenses balance is relative to its annual operating expenses. We'll assume that the company's Prepaid Expenses in this example equals 5 weeks of its annual operating expenses. Previously (page 37) we computed that the operating expenses per week are $18,000. So the Prepaid Expenses balance is computed as follows:

$$\begin{array}{lll} \$18,000 & \times \quad 5 \text{ weeks } = & \$90,000 \\ \text{Operating Expenses} & & \text{Prepaid Expenses} \\ \text{per week} & & \end{array}$$

See in Exhibit D(9) that $90,000 is the balance of the Prepaid Expenses account.

In summary, the company in the example had to prepay more than one month of its annual operating expenses. This is a demand on cash during the year, in the amount of $90,000. If the manager could have reduced these prepayments to, say, only 3 weeks of the annual operating expenses (instead of 5 weeks in the example), the Prepaid Expenses would have been only $54,000 ($18,000 operating expenses per week × 3 weeks = $54,000). This would have reduced the demand on cash by $36,000 ($90,000 actual balance − $54,000 = $36,000 less balance).

On the other hand, if prepayments had been 2 weeks higher, say 7 weeks instead of the 5 weeks in the example, the cash demand would have been $36,000 more. The cash flow impact of Prepaid Expenses is explained further in Chapter 14.

**BALANCE SHEET
AT END OF FIRST YEAR**

Cash		$ 162
Accounts Receivable		486
Inventory		702
Prepaid Expenses		90
Machinery, Equipment, Furniture, and Fixtures	$464	
Accumulated Depreciation	(116)	
Undepreciated Cost		348
Total Assets		$1,788
Accounts Payable:		
Inventory	$216	
Operating Expenses	54	$ 270
Accrued Expenses:		
Operations	$108	
Interest	9	117
Income Tax Payable		30
Short-Term Notes Payable		220
Long-Term Notes Payable		300
Paid-In Capital		701
Retained Earnings		150
Total Liabilities & Stockholders' Equity		$1,788

INCOME STATEMENT FOR FIRST YEAR

Sales Revenue		$4,212
Cost of Goods Sold		2,808
Gross Profit		$1,404
Operating Expenses	$936	
Depreciation Expense	116	
		1,052
Operating Earnings		$ 352
Interest Expense		52
Earnings before Tax		$ 300
Income Tax Expense		150
Net Income		$ 150

CASH FLOW STATEMENT FOR FIRST YEAR

Cash Flow from Operations		
Net Income (from Income Statement)		$ 150
Negative Cash Flow Factors:		
Accounts Receivable Increase	$486	
Inventory Increase	702	
Prepaid Expenses Increase	90	($1,278)
Positive Cash Flow Factors:		
Depreciation	$116	
Accounts Payable Increase	270	
Accrued Expenses Increase	117	
Income Tax Payable Increase	30	$ 533
Cash Flow from Operations		($ 595)
Cash from Financing		
Short-Term Borrowing	$220	
Long-Term Borrowing	300	
Capital Stock Issue	701	1,221
Uses of Cash		
Cash Dividends to Stockholders	– 0 –	
Purchases of Long-Lived Assets	$464	(464)
Increase in Cash during Year		$ 162

10

PROPERTY, PLANT, & EQUIPMENT

DEPRECIATION

ACCUMULATED DEPRECIATION

A Brief Review of Expense Accounting

By now you should have sensed the basic logic of expense accounting. Expenses are not necessarily recorded when they happen to be paid; expenses are not recorded on a cash basis. Expenses are recorded either on a *matching of costs with sales revenues* basis or on a *cost of period* basis. Each basis is explained briefly here:

1. *Matching of costs with sales revenue basis* — cost of goods sold expense, sales commissions expense, and all other expenses directly identifiable with making sales are recorded in the same time period as the sales revenue. The purpose is to match these costs with related sales revenue to get the correct measure of profit from sales.

2. *Cost of period basis* — many expenses are not directly identifiable with particular sales, such as office employees' salaries, rent of building space, data processing and record-keeping, legal and audit, insurance, interest on bor-rowed money, and many more. Nondirect expenses are just as necessary as direct expenses. But there is no way to match them with individual sales. So the nondirect expenses are recorded in the period in which benefit or use to the operations of the business takes place. For example, $1/12$ of the annual fire insurance premium is allocated to each month, office supplies are expensed in the month used, and so on.

The timing of expense recordings to match the expense with the correct sales revenue or to put the expense in the correct time period involves the use of asset and liability accounts. We have already discussed the use of Inventory and Prepaid Expenses for this purpose, as well as the Accounts Payable and Accrued Expenses liabilities. One type of asset not yet discussed is *property, plant, and equipment*, which we now turn to.

Depreciation Expense

In this example the company rents its real estate (land and buildings). Each month the business pays rent and charges the amount to expense because the company receives the use of the space in that month. The company owns the other long-lived assets needed in its operations.

For example, this company owns desks, cash registers, a computer system, trucks, display cabinets, shelving, various machines and tools, and so on. These several different assets are lumped together and reported in one account called *Machinery, Equipment, Furniture, and Fixtures*, which has a balance of $464,000 at the end of the first year. See Exhibit D(10); also, you may want to refer to Exhibit B on page 10 again, which shows the complete format of a classified Balance Sheet. (If this company owned land and buildings, these long-lived assets also would be placed in the Property, Plant, & Equipment section of the Balance Sheet.)

Long-lived assets are used several years, but eventually they either wear out or otherwise lose their usefulness to the business. In short, these assets have a limited life span of business (economic) usefulness. For instance, a typewriter will be disposed of sometime. It won't last forever.

The cost of the typewriter is prorated over each future year of expected use to the business. How many years? This is hardly more than an educated guess. As a practical matter, the minimum (shortest) lives allowed for federal income tax purposes usually are the useful life estimates adopted by a business.

Different types of assets have different allowable life estimates. Recent changes in the federal tax law allow "long-lived" assets to be depreciated over either 3 or 5 years, depending on which type they are. So, in this example we'll assume an average life of 4 years. Depreciation is computed as follows:

$464,000	×	¼	=	$116,000
Machinery, equipment, furniture, and fixtures at original cost		(4 year useful life estimate of all fixed assets)		Depreciation Expense for the year

See the connection in Exhibit D(10). The so-called straight-line (equal amount per year) depreciation method is being assumed here. Depreciation is discussed further in Chapter 22.

The amount of depreciation expense charged to each year is relatively arbitrary compared to other expenses. One reason is that the useful life estimates are arbitrary. For a 12-months' insurance policy, there's little doubt that the total premium cost should be allocated over exactly 12 months. But long-lived assets present much more difficult problems. For an office desk, or display shelving, file cabinets, computers, or typewriters: how long will these assets be used?

Given the inherent problems of estimating useful lives, financial statement readers are well advised to keep in mind the consequences of wrong estimates. If the useful life estimates are too short, depreciation expense each year is too high. In fact, useful life estimates are generally too short. Accountants, with the blessing of the Internal Revenue Law, favor this more conservative approach.

The Accumulated Depreciation Account

The amount of depreciation expense each year is not recorded as a decrease in the asset account directly. Instead, each year the amount of depreciation expense is added to the Accumulated Depreciation account. The balance in this account is deducted from the original cost of the assets [see Exhibit D(10)]. The remainder – $348,000 in this example – is called the *book value*. It's the undepreciated part of the assets' original cost, or future depreciation expense if you would.

The Accumulated Depreciation balance is the total depreciation recorded in this and previous years. In Exhibit D(10) only 1 year of depreciation expense has been recorded because the business has been in operation only one year. So the Accumulated Depreciation account shows only the first year's depreciation amount. At the end of the second year, this account will show the total of the first and second years' depreciation expense.

Book Values of Long-Lived Assets Compared with Their Replacement Costs

After several years the original cost of the long-lived assets reported in a company's Balance Sheet will be quite low compared to the current replacement costs of equivalent new long-lived assets. Inflation has hit these asset costs as much or more than everything else. The original cost amounts reported in a Balance Sheet are not meant to be indicators of the current replacement costs of the assets.

When looking ahead, managers, creditors, and investors should realize that the future replacement costs of these assets will be much higher than the historical costs reported in the Balance Sheet. For management purposes every year or two it's

a good idea to make an estimate of the current replacement costs of the business' long-lived operating assets. This does not and should not lead to a write-up of the assets in the Balance Sheet. This would be against generally accepted accounting principles.

Many business managers and many accountants have argued that such assets should be written-up once every year to keep up with inflation, and that the depreciation expense each year should be based on the higher values. So far Congress has rejected this method for federal income tax purposes.

Nevertheless, the matter has been one of very serious and

continuing concern to the accounting profession, even though many doubt the usefulness of such information to investors. Somewhat as an experiment, the rule making body of the accounting profession recently passed a requirement that large (indeed, very large!) public corporations must provide *supplementary* information about the current costs of their long-lived operating assets. How useful is this information? It's still too early to tell for sure.

BALANCE SHEET
AT END OF FIRST YEAR

Cash		$ 162
Accounts Receivable		486
Inventory		702
Prepaid Expenses		90
Machinery, Equipment, Furniture, and Fixtures	$464	
Accumulated Depreciation	(116)	
Undepreciated Cost		348
Total Assets		$1,788
Accounts Payable:		
Inventory	$216	
Operating Expenses	54	$ 270
Accrued Expenses:		
Operations	$108	
Interest	9	117
Income Tax Payable		30
Short-Term Notes Payable		220
Long-Term Notes Payable		300
Paid-In Capital		701
Retained Earnings		150
Total Liabilities & Stockholders' Equity		$1,788

INCOME STATEMENT FOR FIRST YEAR

Sales Revenue		$4,212
Cost of Goods Sold		2,808
Gross Profit		$1,404
Operating Expenses	$936	
Depreciation Expense	116	1,052
Operating Earnings		$ 352
Interest Expense		52
Earnings before Tax		$ 300
Income Tax Expense		150
Net Income		$ 150

CASH FLOW STATEMENT FOR FIRST YEAR

Cash Flow from Operations		
Net Income (from Income Statement)		$ 150
Negative Cash Flow Factors:		
Accounts Receivable Increase	$486	
Inventory Increase	702	
Prepaid Expenses Increase	90	($1,278)
Positive Cash Flow Factors:		
Depreciation	$116	
Accounts Payable Increase	270	
Accrued Expenses Increase	117	
Income Tax Payable Increase	30	$ 533
Cash Flow from Operations		($ 595)
Cash from Financing		
Short-Term Borrowing	$220	
Long-Term Borrowing	300	
Capital Stock Issue	701	1,221
Uses of Cash		
Cash Dividends to Stockholders	– 0 –	
Purchases of Long-Lived Assets	$464	(464)
Increase in Cash during Year		$ 162

11

INTEREST EXPENSE
↓
ACCRUED EXPENSES (PAYABLE)

It's a rare business that doesn't borrow money, in addition to having Accounts Payable and Accrued Expenses liabilities. A *note* (or similar legal instrument) is signed when borrowing; hence the liabilities from borrowing are called *Notes Payable.* One main difference is that interest is paid on borrowed money of course, whereas no interest is paid on Accounts Payable and Accrued Expenses. Notes Payable are always reported separate from non-interest-bearing liablities in the Balance Sheet.

Interest is a charge per day for the use of borrowed money. Every day the money is borrowed means that more interest is owed. The ratio of interest to the amount borrowed is called the interest rate, and always is stated as a percent. Percent means "per-hundred." If you borrow $100,000 for one year and pay $12,000 interest, the rate (ratio) of interest is: $12,000 interest ÷ $100,000 borrowed = $12 per $100, or 12%. Interest rates are stated as annual rates, even though the term of borrowing is shorter or longer than 1 year.

Interest is reported as a separate expense in the Income Statement. It's not the size of interest relative to other expenses, but its special nature that requires this separate disclosure. Interest is a financial cost as opposed to an operating cost; interest depends on the financial policies of the business regarding borrowing, not on its methods of operations.

When interest is paid *depends.* On short-term notes (less than 1 year periods) interest is paid in one sum at the maturity date of the note, which is the last day of the loan period. On longer-term notes, say for 5 or 10 years, interest is paid usually every 6 months, although monthly or quarterly interest payments are not unheard of. On both short-term and long-term notes there is a lag, or delay in paying interest. But the interest expense should be recorded for all days the money was borrowed.

The accumulated amount of unpaid interest expense at the end of the accounting period is recorded in Accrued Expenses, which is a liability account. In this example the year's total interest expense is $52,000, or $1000 per week. Due to the lag in paying interest, 9 weeks expense is unpaid at year-end, so:

$1000   × 9 weeks = $9000
Interest Expense   Accrued
per week   Expenses

See the connection in Exhibit D(11).

You'll notice that Accrued Expenses now has a total balance of $117,000 — the $9000 unpaid interest expense plus the $108,000 unpaid operating expenses discussed earlier in Chapter 8.

EXHIBIT D(12)

BALANCE SHEET
AT END OF FIRST YEAR

Cash		$ 162
Accounts Receivable		486
Inventory		702
Prepaid Expenses		90
Machinery, Equipment, Furniture, and Fixtures	$464	
Accumulated Depreciation	(116)	
Undepreciated Cost		348
Total Assets		$1,788
Accounts Payable:		
Inventory	$216	
Operating Expenses	54	$ 270
Accrued Expenses:		
Operations	$108	
Interest	9	117
Income Tax Payable		30
Short-Term Notes Payable		220
Long-Term Notes Payable		300
Paid-In Capital		701
Retained Earnings		150
Total Liabilities & Stockholders' Equity		$1,788

INCOME STATEMENT FOR FIRST YEAR

Sales Revenue		$4,212
Cost of Goods Sold		2,808
Gross Profit		$1,404
Operating Expenses	$936	
Depreciation Expense	116	1,052
Operating Earnings		$ 352
Interest Expense		52
Earnings before Tax		$ 300
Income Tax Expense		150
Net Income		$ 150

CASH FLOW STATEMENT FOR FIRST YEAR

Cash Flow from Operations		
Net Income (from Income Statement)		$ 150
Negative Cash Flow Factors:		
Accounts Receivable Increase	$486	
Inventory Increase	702	
Prepaid Expenses Increase	90	($1,278)
Positive Cash Flow Factors:		
Depreciation	$116	
Accounts Payable Increase	270	
Accrued Expenses Increase	117	
Income Tax Payable Increase	30	$ 533
Cash Flow from Operations		($ 595)
Cash from Financing		
Short-Term Borrowing	$220	
Long-Term Borrowing	300	
Capital Stock Issue	701	1,221
Uses of Cash		
Cash Dividends to Stockholders	– 0 –	
Purchases of Long-Lived Assets	$464	(464)
Increase in Cash during Year		$ 162

12

INCOME TAX EXPENSE

$\downarrow$

INCOME TAX PAYABLE

Refer to the connection in Exhibit D(12) between Income Tax Expense in the Income Statement with Income Tax Payable in the Balance Sheet.

The business in our example is incorporated. A corporation, being a separate entity (person) in the eyes of the law, has several legal advantages. However, profit-motivated business corporations have one serious disadvantage — they are subject to federal and state income taxes as a separate entity.

The term "subject to" here is used deliberately. First, a corporation must earn a taxable income to be taxed. Second, there are many provisions and options in the tax laws that result in paying less tax, or perhaps no income tax at all in a given year.

It takes hundreds of pages in the federal law to define *taxable income*. Then it takes many more pages to define how to compute the income tax owed on the amount of taxable income. Capital gains are treated differently than "ordinary" taxable income. Investment tax credits reduce the final amount of tax paid. Losses of one year can be offset against taxable income of other years. Surely you know how complex is the federal income tax on business corporations (as well as individuals). Also, most states impose an income tax on corporations doing business in their boundaries.

This is not the place to explain taxation of business profit. To simplify, therefore, two key assumptions are made in this example.

First Simplifying Assumption

The company's accounting methods used to determine its annual taxable income are the same methods used to prepare its financial statements. There are no differences in recording its sales revenue and no differences in recording its expenses. Also, it is assumed that all recorded expenses are fully deductible for income tax purposes. Generally speaking, this harmony of income tax and financial statement accounting methods is true. Yet, many differences are permitted. To minimize its taxable income a corporation may use more conservative accounting methods in its tax returns than in its financial statements. This would lead us into very technical and complex detours from the main discussion.

Second Simplifying Assumption

The combined federal and state income tax rate is 50% of taxable income. This is a reasonable approximation that avoids several tax computation steps. For instance, reduced federal tax rates apply on the taxable income layers below $100,001; and, state tax is deductible for federal purposes and federal tax is deductible for state purposes.

Given these two assumptions, the corporation's taxable income is $300,000 [see Exhibit D(12)], and its total income tax for the year is:

$$\begin{array}{llll} \$300,000 & \times\ 50\% & = \$150,000 \\ \text{Taxable Income} & \text{combined federal and} & \text{Income Tax Expense} \\ & \text{state income tax rate} & \text{for year} \end{array}$$

Corporations have to make progress payments on their income tax as they go through the year. Simply speaking, at the start of the year a corporation makes an estimate of what its taxable income will be for the coming year. Based on this estimated taxable income, the corporation estimates its income tax for the year. The corporation has to make installment payments during the year, totaling 80% of its estimated tax for the year.

If less than 80% is paid during the year, penalties on the amount of underpayment may be imposed. However, there are several technical provisions and exceptions that may come into play such that the business escapes any penalty. It is not unrealistic to assume that a business paid in less than 80% during the year. However, we'll assume that the business in this example paid 80% and thus 20% is still owed to the Internal Revenue Service at year-end:

$150,000	× 20% balance owed	= $30,000
Income Tax Expense	on total income tax	Income Tax
for year	for the year	Payable

See the connection in Exhibit D(12).

**BALANCE SHEET
AT END OF FIRST YEAR**

Cash		$ 162
Accounts Receivable		486
Inventory		702
Prepaid Expenses		90
Machinery, Equipment, Furniture, and Fixtures	$464	
Accumulated Depreciation	(116)	
Undepreciated Cost		348
Total Assets		$1,788
Accounts Payable:		
Inventory	$216	
Operating Expenses	54	$ 270
Accrued Expenses:		
Operations	$108	
Interest	9	117
Income Tax Payable		30
Short-Term Notes Payable		220
Long-Term Notes Payable		300
Paid-In Capital		701
Retained Earnings		150
Total Liabilities & Stockholders' Equity		$1,788

INCOME STATEMENT FOR FIRST YEAR

Sales Revenue		$4,212
Cost of Goods Sold		2,808
Gross Profit		$1,404
Operating Expenses	$936	
Depreciation Expense	116	1,052
Operating Earnings		$ 352
Interest Expense		52
Earnings before Tax		$ 300
Income Tax Expense		150
Net Income		$ 150

CASH FLOW STATEMENT FOR FIRST YEAR

Cash Flow from Operations		
Net Income (from Income Statement)		$ 150
Negative Cash Flow Factors:		
Accounts Receivable Increase	$486	
Inventory Increase	702	
Prepaid Expenses Increase	90	($1,278)
Positive Cash Flow Factors:		
Depreciation	$116	
Accounts Payable Increase	270	
Accrued Expenses Increase	117	
Income Tax Payable Increase	30	$ 533
Cash Flow from Operations		($ 595)
Cash from Financing		
Short-Term Borrowing	$220	
Long-Term Borrowing	300	
Capital Stock Issue	701	1,221
Uses of Cash		
Cash Dividends to Stockholders	– 0 –	
Purchases of Long-Lived Assets	$464	(464)
Increase in Cash during Year		$ 162

13

NET INCOME (PROFIT)

$\downarrow$

RETAINED EARNINGS

See the connection in Exhibit D(13) linking net income from the Income Statement to Retained Earnings in the Balance Sheet. Net income increases the balance in the Retained Earnings account. As explained before, but worth repeating here, net income is the final profit after deducting all expenses from sales revenue.

Now a very important question: at year-end where is net income? The answer to this question requires that we build on the discussion in previous chapters. Sales revenue results in asset increases, and expenses result in asset decreases or liability increases. Sales revenue and expenses affect virtually all the assets and most of the liabilities of a business, as explained in previous chapters.

Exhibit E presents a summary of the increases and decreases of the company's assets and liabilities resulting from its sales revenue and expenses for the year. The amounts of these increases and decreases are precisely the main points discussed in earlier chapters, except for the decrease of Cash. The cash flow analysis of net income is extremely important to business managers, creditors, and investors, and is discussed fully in the next chapter. For now you might refer to the earlier discussion in Chapter 1 (page 5) which shows the summary of cash receipts

EXHIBIT E—ASSET AND LIABILITY CHANGES CAUSED BY NET INCOME (OPERATING) ACTIVITIES

Asset Changes		
Cash	−$595,000	
Accounts Receivable	+ 486,000	
Inventory	+ 702,000	
Prepaid Expenses	+ 90,000	
Machinery, Equipment, Furniture, and Fixtures	− 116,000	
Total Asset Increases		$567,000
Liability Changes		
Accounts Payable	+$270,000	
Accrued Expenses	+ 117,000	
Income Tax Payable	+ 30,000	
Total Liability Increases		417,000
Net Income (Asset Increases less Liability Increases)		$150,000

from sales and cash disbursements for expenses. Notice that the bottom line of that cash flow summary is a $595,000 decrease in cash; in Exhibit E Cash also shows a $595,000 decrease.

The main point here is that net income consists of a mix of increases and decreases in several asset and liability accounts—as shown in Exhibit E. Net income is not simply money in the bank. In fact cash decreased during the first year from the company's net income making operations.

Dividends, if and when paid, are recorded as decreases in Retained Earnings. But because of the cash decrease from net income, the company did not distribute any cash dividends to its stockholders. Thus Retained Earnings increased by the entire $150,000 amount of net income. (See the line of connection in Exhibit D(13), which indicates that no cash dividends were paid.)

In short, the balance in Retained Earnings is just that—the amount of net income earned *and* retained by the business. Sometimes it's called Undistributed Net Income, or Undistributed Earnings, though the title Retained Earnings is much more common.*

It's very important to understand that Retained Earnings is *not* an asset. Nor does it indicate how much cash or how much of any other particular asset the company has. Think of Retained Earnings as a balance account, the last weight you put on the scales to make for a perfect balance.

Let's return to Exhibit E again, which summarizes the asset and liability changes from net income for the year. To sum-

*God forbid, but occasionally you still see the term "Earned Surplus" (instead of Retained Earnings). This title is especially confusing and as outmoded as the Model T.

marize even further, net income can be put as follows:

$$\underset{\text{increases in assets}}{\$567,000} - \underset{\text{increases in liabilities}}{\$417,000} = \underset{\text{net income}}{\$150,000}$$

Without Retained Earnings in the Balance Sheet, net income would cause an imbalance, like a teeter-totter out of balance:

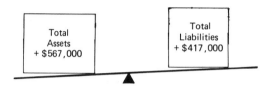

With Retained Earnings there is a balance:

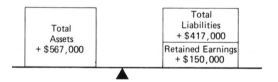

Retained Earnings does more than keep the Balance Sheet in a condition of equality. It keeps track of how much of total owners' (stockholders') equity was earned and retained by the business versus how much capital has been invested from time to time by the owners (which is recorded in the other owners' equity account). Legally these two sources of owners' equity must be separated.

Looking at the Retained Earnings balance is like looking into a mirror. The real profit earned by a business is found in the assets less the liabilities of the business. Retained Earnings is only the image in the mirror (in one amount).

BALANCE SHEET
AT END OF FIRST YEAR

Cash		$ 162
Accounts Receivable		486
Inventory		702
Prepaid Expenses		90
Machinery, Equipment, Furniture, and Fixtures	$464	
Accumulated Depreciation	(116)	
Undepreciated Cost		348
Total Assets		$1,788
Accounts Payable:		
Inventory	$216	
Operating Expenses	54	$ 270
Accrued Expenses:		
Operations	$108	
Interest	9	117
Income Tax Payable		30
Short-Term Notes Payable		220
Long-Term Notes Payable		300
Paid-In Capital		701
Retained Earnings		150
Total Liabilities & Stockholders' Equity		$1,788

INCOME STATEMENT FOR FIRST YEAR

Sales Revenue		$4,212
Cost of Goods Sold		2,808
Gross Profit		$1,404
Operating Expenses	$936	
Depreciation Expense	116	1,052
Operating Earnings		$ 352
Interest Expense		52
Earnings before Tax		$ 300
Income Tax Expense		150
Net Income		$ 150

CASH FLOW STATEMENT FOR FIRST YEAR

Cash Flow from Operations

Net Income (from Income Statement)		$ 150
Negative Cash Flow Factors:		
Accounts Receivable Increase	$486	
Inventory Increase	702	
Prepaid Expenses Increase	90	($1,278)
Positive Cash Flow Factors:		
Depreciation	$116	
Accounts Payable Increase	270	
Accrued Expenses Increase	117	
Income Tax Payable Increase	30	$ 533
Cash Flow from Operations		($ 595)

Cash from Financing

Short-Term Borrowing	$220	
Long-Term Borrowing	300	
Capital Stock Issue	701	1,221

Uses of Cash

Cash Dividends to Stockholders		– 0 –
Purchases of Long-Lived Assets	$464	(464)
Increase in Cash during Year		$ 162

14

CASH FLOW ANALYSIS
OF OPERATIONS

Making sales and controlling expenses is a demanding task, to say the least. However, earning an adequate profit is not enough. Managing cash is just as important. Enough cash must be available *when needed*. Earning a good profit does not necessarily guarantee an adequate cash flow when needed.

In short, business managers have a double duty: to earn profit, and to convert the profit into cash reasonably soon. Waiting too long to turn profit into cash reduces the value of the profit.

Managers use the Income Statement to review and evaluate profit performance, and to prepare the profit plan for the coming year. Likewise, managers should use the *Cash Flow Statement* to review cash flows for the year just ended, and to prepare the cash flow budget for the coming year. Not to plan cash flows would invite disaster.

Exhibit D(14) presents the company's Cash Flow Statement for its first year of business, on the right side of its Balance Sheet. The enclosed area of the Cash Flow Statement is discussed in this chapter, and the remainder of the statement is discussed in the next chapter.

The company's Cash Flow Statement begins with an analysis of the cash flow effects from operations, which are all those activities directly a part of making profit (net income). In other words, operations refers to those transactions involved in making sales and incurring expenses.

Net income is earned when sales revenue and expenses are recorded. These recordings, in large part, are made either before or after the related cash flows occur. Over a long time, say 10 to 15 years, the total increase in cash would be very close to the total net income earned. But in any one year the cash flow can be considerably less or more than the amount of net income reported in the Income Statement for that year.

Cash flow analysis of operations starts with the amount of net income from the Income Statement. However, changes in operating assets and operating liabilities during the year usually cause cash flow from operations to be quite different from net income for the year – which is certainly true in this case! Please note in Exhibit D(14) the lines extending from the operating assets and operating liabilities into the Cash Flow Statement.

Negative cash flow factors are those changes in operating assets or liabilities that decrease the cash flow from operations (net income). Positive cash flow factors are those changes that increase cash flow.

Accounts Receivable increased $486,000 during the year, which means that $486,000 of its sales revenue for the year had not been received in cash by year-end. Only $3,726,000 of the company's sales revenue was actually collected in cash ($4,212,000 sales revenue less $486,000 Accounts Receivable = $3,726,000 cash received). So the $486,000 increase in Accounts Receivable during the year is a negative cash flow factor.

Next, Inventory increased $702,000 during the year. In addition to its cost of goods sold during the year, the company made inventory purchases of $702,000 to build up its stock of goods held for sale. These purchases have to be paid for, of course. The $702,000 is an additional demand on cash, so it is also a negative cash flow factor. (Part of the inventory purchases are still unpaid at year-end; the Accounts Payable for these are considered later.)

Prepaid Expenses increased $90,000 during the year. In addition to its operating expenses, the company had to prepay $90,000 of next year's expenses, which is the ending balance of Prepaid Expenses. This $90,000 is an additional demand on cash during the year, and this is a negative cash flow factor.

To this point, things look pretty bad. The three negative

cash flow factors add up to $1,278,000 – see Exhibit D(14) again. However, on the other side of the coin as it were, the company did not have to pay out in cash the entire amount of expenses reported in the Income Statement. These unpaid expenses are the positive cash flow factors next shown in the Cash Flow Statement.

First of all, depreciation expense is not a cash outlay. See Exhibit D(14) again. Notice that the depreciation expense increases the Accumulated Depreciation account, which is deducted from the asset account. The asset account, not Cash, is decreased. So, depreciation expense is a positive cash flow factor.*

The earlier chapters explain that three liabilities are directly affected by the expenses of the business – Accounts Payable, Accrued Expenses, and Income Tax Payable. An increase in an operating liability during the year means that cash was not paid out by the amount of the increase.

The increases for each liability are their year-end balances because this example is for the first year of business. (There were no liabilities at the start of the year.) The year-end balances are the unpaid amounts resulting from the expenses during the year. Cash payments of these amounts were avoided during the year; cash will not be paid until next year.

To sum up: Starting with $150,000 net income, deducting the $1,278,000 negative cash flow factors, and adding the

*You may see a figure called "cash flow from net income" that is simply the net income amount plus the depreciation expense for the period. But this is not really cash flow from operations. Cash flow analysis must look at all the assets and liabilities affected by sales revenue and expenses.

$533,000 positive cash flow factors, gives the *negative* $595,000 cash flow from operations – see Exhibit D(14).

By the way, you should notice that this $595,000 is the same as originally given in the cash receipts and payments summary in Chapter 1 on page 5. The cash summary certainly is *not* the correct way to measure profit. But it does show the cash receipts and payments from sales and expenses for the period.

Exhibit F shown on page 72 reconciles the cash flow amounts given in Chapter 1 with the amounts in the Income Statement. This exhibit is a powerful tool of explanation. It shows what's wrong with the cash basis for profit measurement. For example, the cash basis ignores Accounts Receivable at year-end from sales made but not yet collected. Also, Exhibit F is an excellent way to focus attention on the key assumptions we make in accounting for profit.

For instance, we assume that the Accounts Receivable will be collected. We assume that Inventory will be sold. We assume that the business will continue in operation to take advantage of its Prepaid Expenses and its long-lived assets. We assume that Accounts Payable, Accrued Expenses, and Income Tax Payable will be paid at the amounts recorded.

If any of the assumptions are subject to doubt, profit measurement becomes more of a problem. For example, not all the Accounts Receivable may be collected. So we should allow for some bad debts. Perhaps some of the Inventory will not be sold, or sold at greatly reduced prices. So we should write-down Inventory to record its loss of value. These accounting problems are the next step in learning financial statement accounting methods, which go beyond the coverage of this book.

To return to the cash flow impact of net income: there was a cash outflow of $595,000 during the first year from net income

EXHIBIT F—CASH FLOWS RECONCILED WITH ACCRUAL BASIS OF NET INCOME
(FOR FIRST YEAR OF BUSINESS)

	Cash Flows	Differences and Brief Explanation*	Accrual Basis
Sales	$3,726,000	+ $486,000 Accounts Receivable (sales were made this period even though cash will not be collected until next period)	$4,212,000
Goods sold	(3,294,000)	− $702,000 Inventory (goods have not been sold yet but will be next period)	
		+ $216,000 Accounts Payable (goods have been purchased but not paid for by end of year)	(2,808,000)
Operating expenses	(864,000)	− $ 90,000 Prepaid Expenses (costs paid for that will benefit next period)	
		+ $ 54,000 Accounts Payable (costs that benefited this period but will not be paid until next period)	
		+ $108,000 Accrued Expenses (estimated amount of accumulated costs that benefited this period but won't be paid until next period)	(936,000)
Depreciation	— 0 —	+ $116,000 Accumulated Depreciation (decrease in long-lived operating assets to recognize using the resources during this period)	(116,000)
Interest	(43,000)	+ $ 9,000 Accrued Expenses (unpaid interest at year-end for the use of debt during this period)	(52,000)
Income tax	(120,000)	+ $ 30,000 Income Tax Payable (amount still owed on the taxable income earned this period)	(150,000)
Cash Decrease From Operations	($595,000)	Net Income	$ 150,000

*See Exhibit D(14) on page 68

activities. The company had to borrow money and raise capital from its stockholders to cover this $595,000 "pull down" on cash during the year; these sources of capital are discussed in the next chapter.

Such a large negative impact on cash from net income is a one-time first year start-up situation. Recall that the example is for the company's first year of business. In later years net income usually generates an increase in cash, although not necessarily equal to or even close to the amount of net income. Chapter 16 presents the cash flow analysis from net income for the company's second year of business. There is a cash inflow in the second year.

**BALANCE SHEET
AT END OF FIRST YEAR**

CASH FLOW STATEMENT FOR FIRST YEAR

INCOME STATEMENT FOR FIRST YEAR

Sales Revenue		$4,212
Cost of Goods Sold		2,808
Gross Profit		$1,404
Operating Expenses	$936	
Depreciation Expense	116	1,052
Operating Earnings		$ 352
Interest Expense		52
Earnings before Tax		$ 300
Income Tax Expense		150
Net Income		$ 150

Cash		$ 162
Accounts Receivable		486
Inventory		702
Prepaid Expenses		90
Machinery, Equipment, Furniture, and Fixtures	$464	
Accumulated Depreciation	(116)	
Undepreciated Cost		348
Total Assets		$1,788
Accounts Payable:		
Inventory	$216	
Operating Expenses	54	$ 270
Accrued Expenses:		
Operations	$108	
Interest	9	117
Income Tax Payable		30
Short-Term Notes Payable		220
Long-Term Notes Payable		300
Paid-In Capital		701
Retained Earnings		150
Total Liabilities & Stockholders' Equity		$1,788

Cash Flow from Operations

Net Income (from Income Statement)		$ 150
Negative Cash Flow Factors:		
Accounts Receivable Increase	$486	
Inventory Increase	702	
Prepaid Expenses Increase	90	($1,278)
Positive Cash Flow Factors:		
Depreciation	$116	
Accounts Payable Increase	270	
Accrued Expenses Increase	117	
Income Tax Payable Increase	30	$ 533
Cash Flow from Operations		($ 595)

Cash from Financing

Short-Term Borrowing	$220	
Long-Term Borrowing	300	
Capital Stock Issue	701	1,221

Uses of Cash

Cash Dividends to Stockholders	– 0 –	
Purchases of Long-Lived Assets	$464	(464)
Increase in Cash during Year		$ 162

15

**OTHER SOURCES AND
USES OF CASH**

During its first year of business our company had to build up its Accounts Receivable, Inventory, and Prepaid Expenses from a zero base at the start of the year to their year-end balances. In part these sizable increases could be financed by corresponding increases in its current operating liabilities. But only in part. The excess had to be financed from other sources. Also, the company needed a working cash balance.

Obviously the company had to raise a good deal of capital. The remainder of the Cash Flow Statement reports the sources of capital raised during the year, and the uses of this capital [see Exhibit D(15)].

In brief, the company borrowed $520,000−$220,000 on short-term notes and $300,000 on long-term notes. (Some of the short-term notes were paid and replaced by new short-term notes during the year, but this turnover needn't concern us.) And the stockholders invested $701,000 at the start of the year, for which they received stock shares from the corporation. Together the debt and equity sources of capital provided $1,221,000.

Decisions on how to finance a business, concerning the mix of equity (stock), short-term debt, long-term debt, and other types of securities are financial management questions, not financial statement accounting matters as such. Needless to say, there are many factors and alternatives that have to be considered, that are far beyond the scope of this book.

The company used $464,000 of the total capital to purchase various long-lived operating assets, leaving $757,000 for other purposes. The preceding chapter explains that the profit making activities of the company were not a source of cash during the first year, but, instead, required the *use* of $595,00 cásh. Subtracting this $595,000 from the $757,000 leaves $162,000 available. The company could have paid cash dividends to its stockholders, but did not. Hence, the $162,000 should be the Cash balance at year-end. Indeed, if you'll look at Exhibit D(15) again, you'll see that the ending Cash balance is $162,000. So we have accounted for all the sources and uses of cash during the year.

At this point, you should follow each line of connection from the Cash Flow Statement to its Balance Sheet destination in Exhibit D(15). This completes the Balance Sheet. All items in the Balance Sheet have been explained.

In summary, the Cash Flow Statement deserves as much attention and study as the Income Statement and Balance Sheet. Very few companies have so much cash that they can ignore cash flows period by period. Cash flows directly affect the ability of the company to pay its debts on time, and to pay cash dividends from net income. So, creditors and investors are (or should be) as interested in cash flows as managers.

16

IMPACT OF GROWTH VERSUS NO-GROWTH ON CASH FLOW

In previous chapters we've analyzed the company's financial statements for its first, or start-up, year of business. The first year is the natural starting point for introducing financial statements, which also brings out the special cash flow demands during the first year. Once over the first-year hump, however, managing cash flow and financial condition take on a different character.

In analyzing cash flow from operations for the first year of business we concentrated on end-of-year effects. For example, Accounts Receivable was $486,000 at the end of the first year; this means total cash receipts from customers were this much less than sales revenue for the first year. In the second year of business (and succeeding years) we must consider beginning-of-year effects also. For example, the $486,000 Accounts Receivable at the end of the first year carries forward as the beginning balance at the start of the second year. The $486,000 is collected during the second year, which adds to cash inflow in year two.

In summary, *both ending and beginning* balances of every asset and every liability affected by sales revenue and expenses have to be considered in determining the cash flow from operations in a continuing year of business (every year after the first year).

Beginning balances, compared with ending balances, have *reverse* effects on cash flow. If the ending balance has a negative effect, the beginning balance has a positive effect—and vice versa. If the ending balance happened to equal the beginning balance there would be a break-even effect. For instance, if the Accounts Receivable ending balance were the same as its beginning balance, cash receipts from customers during the year would be the same as sales revenue for the year.

The No-Growth Case:
A Very Useful Point of Reference

A very useful baseline of reference for understanding the reverse effects between beginning and ending balances is the no-growth case. Exhibit G on page 80 shows the company's financial statements for its second year of business, in exactly the same format as before, on the assumption that sales revenue and all expenses are exactly the same as in the first year.

In essence, we're assuming no inflation, and no changes in the quantity of goods sold nor the "quantities" of all expenses (e.g., number of hours worked by employees, number of kilowatts of electricity used, etc.). Of course, this no-growth, or steady-state assumption is not very realistic. But before we look at the growth case, the no-growth financial statements reveal several valuable points about what happens to cash flow from operations and the financial condition of the business.

In Exhibit G the Income Statement for year two is an exact duplicate of year one. The Balance Sheet at the end of year two is mostly the same as a year ago, with a few important changes discussed in just a minute. But look at the Cash Flow Statement; what a difference from the first year!

Cash *inflow* from operations in year two is $266,000, compared with $595,000 cash *outflow* in year one. The reason for this huge difference, even though sales revenue and expenses are the same both years, is that the company started the second year with sufficient amounts of the current assets and current liabilities required by the sales revenue and expenses, and none increased during the second year. The ending balances are all equal to the beginning balances. Because of the reverse effects of ending and beginning balances, there is a break-even (or zero) effect on cash flow from operations in the year. (See the Cash Flow Statement in Exhibit G.)

In other words, in the no-growth situation a company does not have to increase its Accounts Receivable, Inventory, or Prepaid Expenses. In rough terms, the beginning balances are converted into cash during the year and this cash povides the ending balances, which are the same amounts.

Also, in the no-growth situation a company does not increase its Accounts Payable, Accrued Expenses, or Income Tax Payable. In rough terms, the beginning balances are paid during the year but the ending balances are not paid during the year. The beginning and ending balances of these liabilities are the same amounts; so the "pay-off" of the beginning balances is offset with an equal amount of "borrowing" in the form of the ending balances.

One other asset is affected in recording expenses for the

EXHIBIT G—NO GROWTH CASE FOR SECOND YEAR
(Dollar amounts in thousands)

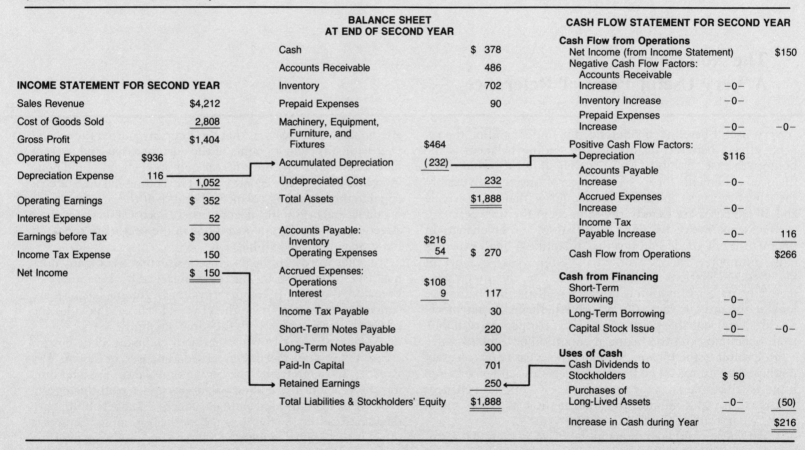

INCOME STATEMENT FOR SECOND YEAR

Sales Revenue		$4,212
Cost of Goods Sold		2,808
Gross Profit		$1,404
Operating Expenses	$936	
Depreciation Expense	116	
		1,052
Operating Earnings		$ 352
Interest Expense		52
Earnings before Tax		$ 300
Income Tax Expense		150
Net Income		$ 150

BALANCE SHEET AT END OF SECOND YEAR

Cash		$ 378
Accounts Receivable		486
Inventory		702
Prepaid Expenses		90
Machinery, Equipment, Furniture, and Fixtures	$464	
Accumulated Depreciation	(232)	
Undepreciated Cost		232
Total Assets		$1,888
Accounts Payable:		
Inventory	$216	
Operating Expenses	54	$ 270
Accrued Expenses:		
Operations	$108	
Interest	9	117
Income Tax Payable		30
Short-Term Notes Payable		220
Long-Term Notes Payable		300
Paid-In Capital		701
Retained Earnings		250
Total Liabilities & Stockholders' Equity		$1,888

CASH FLOW STATEMENT FOR SECOND YEAR

Cash Flow from Operations

Net Income (from Income Statement)		$150
Negative Cash Flow Factors:		
Accounts Receivable Increase	−0−	
Inventory Increase	−0−	
Prepaid Expenses Increase	−0−	−0−
Positive Cash Flow Factors:		
Depreciation	$116	
Accounts Payable Increase	−0−	
Accrued Expenses Increase	−0−	
Income Tax Payable Increase	−0−	116
Cash Flow from Operations		$266

Cash from Financing

Short-Term Borrowing	−0−	
Long-Term Borrowing	−0−	
Capital Stock Issue	−0−	−0−

Uses of Cash

Cash Dividends to Stockholders	$ 50	
Purchases of Long-Lived Assets	−0−	(50)
Increase in Cash during Year		$216

year. The long-lived operating assets were decreased $116,000 by the depreciation expense charged to year two (see Exhibit G). Recording depreciation expense does not decrease cash. Thus the amount of depreciation expense is a positive cash flow factor (the only one!) in the Cash Flow Statement. In rough terms, the company "sold" $116,000 of its long term assets to their customers. Sales prices were set high enough to recover $116,000 of the capital invested in the assets. In this sense, sales revenue in part reimburses the company for the use of these assets in the operations of the business.

There was a "conversion" of $116,000 out of the assets to cash during year two; depreciation can be quite properly thought of in this manner. In addition, the company earned $150,000 net income without any changes in the current assets and current liabilities affected by sales revenue and expenses. So all the $150,000 net income was available in cash *and* $116,000 depreciation was converted into cash. Thus cash flow from net income is $266,000 in the second year.

What happened to the $266,000? The company paid $50,000 cash dividends to its stockholders (see Exhibit G).

The company did *not* replace any of its long-lived operating assets during year two. The assets were purchased new at the start of year one, and none need replacing yet. After a few years of business, however—even in a no-growth situation— the machines, equipment, and so on have to be replaced to maintain the capacity and services provided by the assets.

There were no stock issues and no new borrowing during year two. Therefore, the $266,000 cash inflow from net income (operations) less the $50,000 cash dividends gives a $216,000 increase in cash (see Exhibit G). Cash started the year with a $162,000 balance, so its balance at the end of year two is $378,000.

Also, note that Retained Earnings increased $100,000 during the second year ($150,000 net income less $50,000 dividends), so its balance at the end of year two is $250,000 ($150,000 balance at end of year one plus the $100,000 increase during the second year). What else? Oh, you might also note that the Accumulated Depreciation account now has two years of depreciation expense in it.

The Growth Case: Impacts on Cash Flow

Growth may mean survival, and usually means improvement. Growth is the central strategy of most businesses. But growth puts strains on cash flow, which are the focus of this section.

Instead of the no-growth situation just discussed, assume that the company's sales revenue increased 20% in its second year of business. This would not necessarily mean that each expense would increase exactly 20%—in fact, probably not. But for convenience we'll assume that every expense increased 20% as well, so net income also increased 20%. *And* all the ratios of assets and liabilities and their respective sales revenue or expense are assumed to hold the same in year two.

Given these growth assumptions, the company's financial statements for its second year are shown in Exhibit H (see on page 83).

First of all, notice that cash flow from net income is considerably less than in the no-growth case, even though net income is 20% higher. Net income provided $147,000 cash inflow, compared with $266,000 in the no-growth situation (refer back to Exhibit G on page 80 to check this figure). Accounts Receivable, Inventory, and Prepaid Expenses increased 20% during the year, and these increases put heavy demands on cash.

Offsetting this are the positive cash flow factors: depreciation and the increases in Accounts Payable, Accrued Expenses, and Income Tax Payable. Unless sales revenue and expense increases can be accomplished with little or no increases in the current assets, growth penalizes cash flow. Still, the company did realize $147,000 cash flow from operations—see Exhibit H again.

The company paid $60,000 cash dividends to its stockholders. The cash dividend decision is not an easy one. The first consideration, already discussed, is how much cash inflow was generated from net income. Compared with the $147,000 cash provided from net income, the $60,000 cash dividend looks reasonable. However, *capital expenditures* also have to be considered. That is, how much is needed to replace and/or expand the company's long-lived operating assets during the year?

In this case it's assumed the company increased its long-lived assets by 20% to keep pace with the 20% growth in sales revenue ($464,000 cost from year one $\times$ 20% = $92,800 cost of additional assets in year two). This is a very simple assumption, of course. The relationship of long-lived asset purchases and sales growth is more complex. For instance, in year one the

EXHIBIT H — 20% GROWTH IN SECOND YEAR

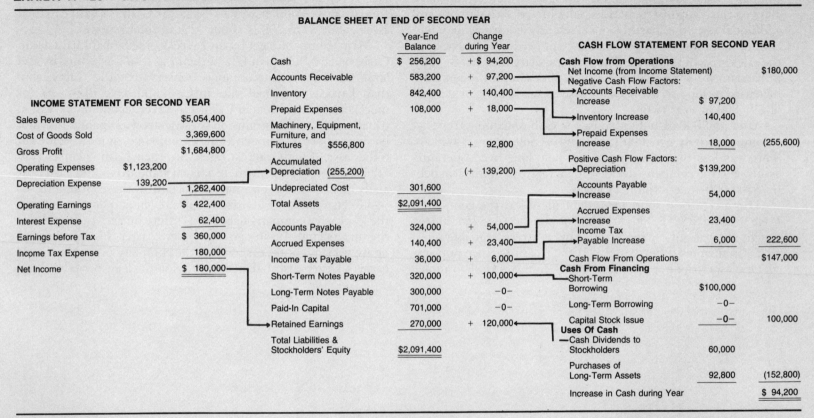

BALANCE SHEET AT END OF SECOND YEAR

INCOME STATEMENT FOR SECOND YEAR

Sales Revenue	$5,054,400
Cost of Goods Sold	3,369,600
Gross Profit	$1,684,800
Operating Expenses	$1,123,200
Depreciation Expense	139,200
	1,262,400
Operating Earnings	$ 422,400
Interest Expense	62,400
Earnings before Tax	$ 360,000
Income Tax Expense	180,000
Net Income	$ 180,000

	Year-End Balance	Change during Year
Cash	$ 256,200	+ $ 94,200
Accounts Receivable	583,200	+ 97,200
Inventory	842,400	+ 140,400
Prepaid Expenses	108,000	+ 18,000
Machinery, Equipment, Furniture, and Fixtures $556,800		+ 92,800
Accumulated Depreciation (255,200)		(+ 139,200)
Undepreciated Cost	301,600	
Total Assets	$2,091,400	
Accounts Payable	324,000	+ 54,000
Accrued Expenses	140,400	+ 23,400
Income Tax Payable	36,000	+ 6,000
Short-Term Notes Payable	320,000	+ 100,000
Long-Term Notes Payable	300,000	–0–
Paid-In Capital	701,000	–0–
Retained Earnings	270,000	+ 120,000
Total Liabilities & Stockholders' Equity	$2,091,400	

CASH FLOW STATEMENT FOR SECOND YEAR

Cash Flow from Operations		
Net Income (from Income Statement)		$180,000
Negative Cash Flow Factors:		
Accounts Receivable Increase	$ 97,200	
Inventory Increase	140,400	
Prepaid Expenses Increase	18,000	(255,600)
Positive Cash Flow Factors:		
Depreciation	$139,200	
Accounts Payable Increase	54,000	
Accrued Expenses Increase	23,400	
Income Tax Payable Increase	6,000	222,600
Cash Flow From Operations		$147,000
Cash From Financing		
Short-Term Borrowing	$100,000	
Long-Term Borrowing	–0–	
Capital Stock Issue	–0–	100,000
Uses Of Cash		
Cash Dividends to Stockholders	60,000	
Purchases of Long-Term Assets	92,800	(152,800)
Increase in Cash during Year		$ 94,200

company may have had excess capacity, which would have allowed the company to increase sales in year two without any additional asset purchases. Conversely, the company may buy considerably more assets this year than needed to provide for the sales growth this year. The extra capacity may not be fully utilized until 3 or 4 years later. But in this example the company increased its long-term operating assets exactly 20%, or at a cost of $92,800 in year two.

After $60,000 cash dividends, the cash remaining from net income was only $87,000 ($147,000 − $60,000 = $87,000). This was less than the cost of the new long-lived operating assets. So, the company decided to increase its short-term debt by $100,000—see Exhibit H again.

The increase in short-term debt increased the company's Cash balance to $256,200 at the end of year two. Is $256,200 too much, about right, or too little? This is a very arguable question. Companies differ widely on their cash balance policies.

One way to look at the question is to compare Cash to annual sales revenue. The $256,200 Cash balance is about 2½ weeks of annual sales. Another way to "size-up" Cash is relative to total assets. The $256,200 is about 12% of total assets.

Many companies get by on 2 weeks or less of annual sales in Cash, or carry less than 12% of their assets in Cash. But, by and large, most companies are more conservative; they carry more than 3 weeks of annual sales in Cash and have 10 to 15% (or more) or of their assets in Cash. However, economic recession usually puts severe strains on these goals. Companies may not be able to borrow as much as they would like, or may decide not to because of high interest rates. So, their Cash balances may fall considerably below their normal standards—and cash flow analysis becomes even more important in these situations.

Given a fairly steady rise of sales revenue month to month, the less cash a company needs as a "safety buffer" to provide for the unexpected. If sales go on a roller coaster through the year or are very cyclical year to year, the company probably should carry a larger cash balance to provide for lean periods.

17

**A QUICK DIVERSION:
THE STATEMENT OF CHANGES
IN FINANCIAL POSITION**

EXHIBIT I—RELATIONSHIP BETWEEN CASH FLOW STATEMENT AND STATEMENT OF CHANGES IN FINANCIAL POSITION

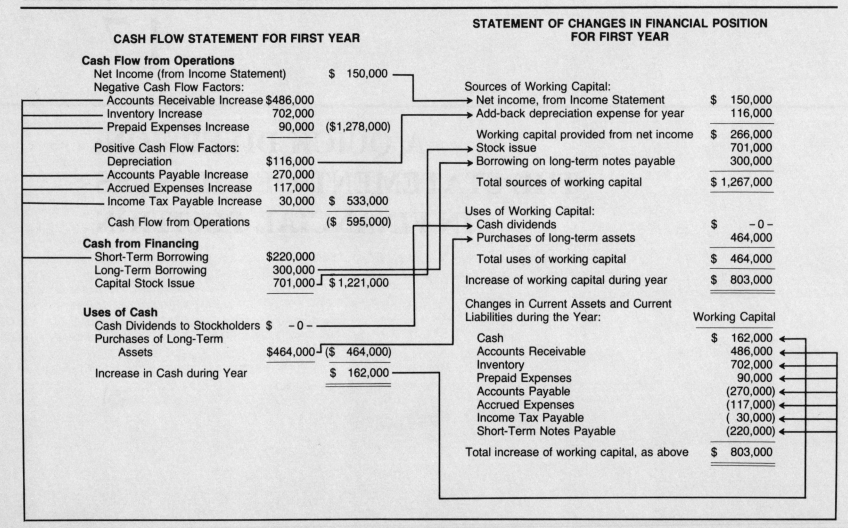

CASH FLOW STATEMENT FOR FIRST YEAR

STATEMENT OF CHANGES IN FINANCIAL POSITION FOR FIRST YEAR

Cash Flow from Operations

Net Income (from Income Statement)		$ 150,000

Negative Cash Flow Factors:

Accounts Receivable Increase	$486,000	
Inventory Increase	702,000	
Prepaid Expenses Increase	90,000	($1,278,000)

Positive Cash Flow Factors:

Depreciation	$116,000	
Accounts Payable Increase	270,000	
Accrued Expenses Increase	117,000	
Income Tax Payable Increase	30,000	$ 533,000
Cash Flow from Operations		($ 595,000)

Cash from Financing

Short-Term Borrowing	$220,000	
Long-Term Borrowing	300,000	
Capital Stock Issue	701,000	$ 1,221,000

Uses of Cash

Cash Dividends to Stockholders	$ – 0 –	
Purchases of Long-Term Assets	$464,000	($ 464,000)
Increase in Cash during Year		$ 162,000

Sources of Working Capital:

Net income, from Income Statement	$ 150,000
Add-back depreciation expense for year	116,000
Working capital provided from net income	$ 266,000
Stock issue	701,000
Borrowing on long-term notes payable	300,000
Total sources of working capital	$ 1,267,000

Uses of Working Capital:

Cash dividends	$ – 0 –
Purchases of long-term assets	464,000
Total uses of working capital	$ 464,000
Increase of working capital during year	$ 803,000

Changes in Current Assets and Current Liabilities during the Year:

	Working Capital
Cash	$ 162,000
Accounts Receivable	486,000
Inventory	702,000
Prepaid Expenses	90,000
Accounts Payable	(270,000)
Accrued Expenses	(117,000)
Income Tax Payable	(30,000)
Short-Term Notes Payable	(220,000)
Total increase of working capital, as above	$ 803,000

In their annual financial reports to creditors and investors, businesses are required to present a financial statement that summarizes their *financing* and *investing* activities during the year. In other words, the business has to report its sources and uses of capital during the year. The Cash Flow Statement discussed at some length in the previous chapters fully satisfies this requirement.

However, you may be surprised to find out that very few companies present a Cash Flow Statement in their external financial reports. Instead, they present a *Statement of Changes in Financial Position*. This statement reports the sources and uses of *working capital* during the period.

Working capital is not cash. Subtract the total of current liabilities from the total of current assets and you have working capital. It's *not* any one asset; it's the difference between current assets and current liabilities.*

Please refer back to the company's Balance Sheet at the end of its first year—see Exhibit B (page 10). In this case the company's working capital would be determined as follows:

Current Assets

Cash	$ 162,000
Accounts Receivable	486,000
Inventory	702,000
Prepaid Expenses	90,000
Total	$1,440,000

*Alternative terms for working capital are *net* working capital, which is clear enough, and the more confusing term *funds*.

Current Liabilities

Accounts Payable	$ 270,000
Accrued Expenses	117,000
Income Tax Payable	30,000
Short-term Notes Payable	220,000
Total	$637,000

Working Capital = $1,440,000 − $637,000 = $803,000

Notice that the short-term notes payable, being classified as a current liability in the Balance Sheet, affects the amount of working capital.

The Statement of Changes in Financial Position is divided into two parts: (1) the *sources* and (2) the *uses* of working capital. Exhibit I on page 86 shows the relationship between the Cash Flow Statement and the Statement of Changes in Financial Position. One focuses on cash flows, and the other focuses on working capital.

The working capital approach has been, by far, the most popular in external financial reports. However, in the last few years more and more dissatisfaction has been voiced over the Statement of Changes in Financial Position and its working capital focus. We'll probably see movement to the Cash Flow Statement in the near future.

18

FOOTNOTES
—THE FINE PRINT
IN EXTERNAL
FINANCIAL REPORTS

Pick up any annual financial report and you'll see the Balance Sheet, Income Statement, and Statement of Changes in Financial Position* Also you'll find a page or more of footnotes. Footnotes provide the "fine print" that goes along with the three principal financial statements.

Managers should never forget that they are responsible for the financial statements and the accompanying footnotes. The footnotes are an integral, inseparable part of the financial report. In fact, financial reports state this on the bottom of each page of the financial statements, usually somewhat as follows:

> The accompanying footnotes to the financial statements are an integral part of these statements.

The auditor's report (see the next chapter) covers the footnotes as well as the financial statements. In short, footnotes are necessary for *adequate disclosure* in external financial reports.

*Remember that the Statement of Changes in Financial Position usually is reported in the external financial report, instead of the Cash Flow Statement.

Two Basic Types of Footnotes

Basically, there are two kinds of footnotes. First, the major *accounting policies* of the business have to be identified and briefly explained. Its cost of goods sold expense method has to be mentioned (see Chapter 21 for discussion of these methods). And its depreciation method has to be mentioned (see Chapter 22). In short, if more than one generally accepted accounting method is allowed, the company's choice of method has to be disclosed. (Chapter 20 discusses the manager's responsibility for these key accounting choices.)

In addition to the key accounting choices of the business, other accounting premises and methods used to prepare the financial statements may be disclosed in footnotes. For example, many larger businesses consist of a family of corporations under the control of one parent corporation. All the separate corporations are consolidated into one set of financial statements. The basis of consolidation is disclosed in a footnote. Also, accounting methods relatively unique to the particular industry or line of business the company is in are disclosed in footnotes.

The second type of footnotes are to provide *additional disclosure* that cannot be placed in the main body of the financial statements. For example, the maturity dates, interest rates, collateral or other security provisions, and other details of the long-term debt of a business are presented in a footnote; annual rentals required under operating leases are given; details regarding any stock option or employee stock ownership plans are spelled out; the amount spent for research and development during the year, if not reported as a separate expense in the Income Statement, may be mentioned.

Further, if there are any major lawsuits in progress against the business, these must be disclosed in a footnote. Details about its employees' retirement and pension plans are also disclosed. The list of possible footnotes is a long one. Many Balance Sheet accounts need additional footnote disclosure, and many liabilities as well.

The Manager's Decision Regarding Footnotes

Managers have to rely on the experts—their chief accounting officer or the CPA auditor—to go through the checklist of footnotes that may be required. Once each required footnote has been identified, the manager should realize that there is still an important decision to make regarding each footnote. There is still a fair amount of management discretion or judgment required regarding just how frank to be, and how much detail to reveal in the footnote.

Clearly the manager should not divulge information that would cause a loss of or decline in any competitive advantage the business now enjoys. Managers don't have to help their competitors—the idea is to help the debtholders and stockholders of the business, to report to them information they are entitled to. But just how much information do the debtholders and stockholders need, or are they legally entitled to? This question is very difficult to answer. Beyond certain minimum basics and details, the extent of "required" or "fair" disclosure in footnotes is *not* at all clear.

Too little disclosure, such as withholding information about a major lawsuit against the business, for instance, would be misleading and the top managers are legally liable for this lack of disclosure. Beyond this "legal minimum," which will be insisted on by the CPA auditors, rules and guidelines are vague and murky. The manager has a fairly broad freedom of choice in how far to go and how frank to be.

Incomprehensible Footnotes:
A Serious Problem to Creditors and Investors

One last point concerns the readability of footnotes. As an author I may be overly sensitive to this, but I think not. Footnote writing sometimes is so poor that you have to suspect that the writing is deliberately bad, to obscure certain information. The rules require footnotes, but the rules do not require that the footnotes be clear and concise so the average financial report reader can understand them.

Frequently the sentence structure of footnotes seems intentionally legalistic and awkward. Terminology is very technical. Many footnotes would get a "F" in an English course.

Poor writing seems more prevalent in footnotes on sensitive matters, such as law suits lost or still in progress, or ventures the business has abandoned with heavy losses. A lack of candor in many footnotes is obvious.

Creditors and stockholders cannot expect managers to expose all the dirty wash of the business in footnotes, or to confess all their bad decisions. But more clarity and honesty certainly would help and would not damage the business.

The stockholders can ask questions at their annual meetings with management and the board of directors. However, managers can be just as evasive in their answers as in the footnotes. Investors can "write their Congressman," but the laws regarding disclosure in financial reports are already on the books.

In short, creditors and investors frequently are stymied by poorly written footnotes. You really have only one choice, and that's to plow slowly through the troublesome footnotes, more than once if necessary. Usually you can tell if the footnote is important enough to deserve this extra effort.

19

THE COST OF
CREDIBILITY
—AUDITS BY CPAs

Why Audits?

Suppose you have invested a lot of money in a business but are not involved in managing the company. You're an "absentee owner." As one of the owners you receive the company's financial reports. The previous chapters have explained how to read and understand the reports. But, how do you know that the financial reports are correct? Can you rely on the reports?

Or, suppose you are a bank loan officer and a business presents its financial report as part of the loan application package. Are the financial statements correct? How do you know?

Or, consider a corporation whose stock shares are traded on the New York Stock Exchange. The market value of the shares depends on the earnings record and other information presented in its financial reports. But, how do the stockholders know that the corporation's financial reports are correct?

The answer to this basic question is to have financial reports audited by *certified public accountants*. Based on the audit the CPA states an opinion on the financial report—an opinion that the business has followed acceptable accounting and disclosure standards in preparing its financial report. This opinion provides additional assurance that the financial report can be relied on by creditors and investors. In short, audits increase the credibility of financial reports.

Who's a certified public accountant? What is an audit of a company's financial statements? Are audits by CPAs required? Even if not required, should a business have its financial statements audited by an independent CPA? What are the limits of audits by CPAs? Do CPAs look for fraud? Will they catch all errors? Should a business use an outside CPA to help prepare its financial statements but *not* have its statements audited? What other services do CPAs offer to business?

These are the main questions addressed in this chapter.

Certified versus
Non-Certified Public Accountants

A person needs to do three things to become a *certified* public accountant (CPA). He or she must earn a college degree with a fairly heavy major (emphasis) in accounting courses. Then the person must pass the national uniform CPA exam. Third, a person needs practical experience working for a CPA firm (in most states).

After all three basic requirements are completed—education, passing the CPA exam, and experience—the person receives the license by the state of residence to practice as a CPA. No one else may hold himself or herself out as a CPA.

The State Boards of Accountancy in all states maintain a directory of those licensed to practice as a CPA in that state.

Those who have not met all the requirements can offer accounting and income tax services to the public, although they seldom do audits. They are called public accountants, or registered accountants. The use of this title and the regulation of non-CPAs vary from state to state. The main reason public accountants are not CPAs is that they have not passed the CPA exam, which is very rigorous and requires thorough preparation to pass.

What Are Audits? What's a Clean Opinion?

First, let's be very clear on one point. We're talking about audits of financial reports by CPAs. There are many other types of audits, such as audits by the Internal Revenue Service of taxpayer returns, audits of federally supported programs by the General Accounting Office, in-house audits by the internal auditors of an organization, and so on. The following discussion concerns audits of financial reports by CPAs for the purpose of the CPA expressing an opinion on the report.

Financial report users are not too concerned about how an audit is done, nor should they be. The bottom line to them is the opinion of the CPA. They should read the opinion carefully, although there is some evidence that most don't. Evidently, many users simply assume that having the financial report audited is, itself, an adequate check, or safeguard. They may assume that the CPA would not be associated with any financial report that is misleading or incorrect. You've heard of "guilt by association" haven't you? Well, you could say that in the case of audits by CPAs there's a kind of reverse approach. Many, perhaps most users of financial reports assume "innocence by association"—if the CPA gives an opinion and thereby is associated with the financial report, then the report must be

OK, or at least not seriously misleading. Doesn't the CPA's opinion constitute a "stamp of approval"?

Actually, such an approach by financial report users is a little naive. The CPA auditing profession has gone to great lengths to define the limits of the audit opinion, and to differentiate between several types of audit opinions.

The best audit opinion is called an *unqualified* opinion, or more popularly a "clean" opinion. Basically, this opinion states that the CPA has no disagreements with the financial report. In other words, the CPA attests that the financial report has been prepared according to generally accepted accounting (and disclosure) principles. (This still leaves management a wide range of choices, as the next chapter explains.) In a clean opinion the CPA auditor says "I don't disagree with the financial report." The CPA might have prepared the report differently; in fact, the CPA might prefer that different accounting methods had been used. All the CPA says in a clean opinion is that the accounting (and disclosure) presented in the financial report is acceptable.

If the CPA cannot give a clean opinion, one or another type of *qualified* opinion is given. A qualified opinion is given if the

CPA disagrees with one of the accounting methods used by the business. Or, if the CPA thinks disclosure is inadequate on some matter a qualified opinion is given. Or, if the company has switched accounting methods the inconsistency is pointed out in a qualified opinion. Or, if there is a major uncertainty (such as a huge lawsuit) hanging over the head of the business a qualified opinion is given. Or, if there is an imminent threat of bankruptcy facing the business a qualified opinion is given.

Qualified opinions spring from many different reasons.

However, such audit opinions do have one thing in common. The CPA must be satisfied that the financial statements taken as a whole are not misleading, even though a qualified opinion is being given. The qualification acts as a warning or as a statement of disagreement by the CPA; this is true. But on the other hand, the CPA still says that, overall, the financial statements and disclosure in the financial report are not misleading. Basically, the CPA says to be a little more careful in reading the financial report when a qualified opinion is given on the report.

Are Audits by CPAs Required?

Publicly-owned corporations whose debt and/or stock securities are traded on a stock exchange or over-the-counter are required by federal securities laws to have their annual financial reports audited by an independent CPA firm. These include more than 10,000 corporations in the United States today.

Beyond this group it is more difficult to generalize about which businesses are legally required to have their financial reports audited by CPAs, either annually or on certain occasions. There may be a legal need for an audit when raising capital through issuing debt or equity securities, even if the securities do not come under federal law. Lawyers should be consulted regarding state corporation and securities laws. Also, as a condition of borrowing money or issuing stock, a business can agree to have its annual financial reports audited.

But there are thousands and thousands of businesses that are not legally required to have their financial statements audited by CPAs. Neither federal nor state laws require the audits, and the businesses have not bound themselves by contract to have audits.

Even if Not Required, Should a Business Have Its Financial Report Audited by an Independent CPA?

Basically, audits by independent CPAs add *credibility* to the financial statements of a business. Audited financial statements have a higher credibility index than unaudited ones.

Two factors may cause the unaudited financial statements of a business to be wrong and seriously misleading:

1. *Honest mistakes* resulting from an inadequate accounting system or an inadequate understanding of accounting principles and financial reporting standards.

2. *Deliberate dishonesty* by a business manager who distorts the amounts reported in the financial statements or withholds important information.

Audits guard against both of these causes of misleading financial statements. Auditors are expert accounting system "detectives," and they thoroughly understand accounting principles and reporting standards. And, being independent of the business, the CPA auditor will not tolerate management dishonesty in the financial statements.

Be warned that the cost of an audit is high. The business manager cannot really bargain over how much auditing will be done. An audit is an audit. The CPA is bound by generally accepted auditing standards (GAAS), which are the authoritative rules in doing audits. There is no such thing as a "bargain basement" audit, or a "quick and dirty, once over lightly" audit. Violations of GAAS can result in legal suits against the CPA, or may damage the CPA's professional reputation.

An audit requires a lot of work before the auditor can express an opinion on the financial statements (including footnotes). This results in the relatively high cost of an audit. The manager has to ask whether the gain in credibility is worth the cost of an audit.

A bank may insist on regular audits as a condition of making loans to a business. Or, those stockholders not directly involved in the day-to-day management of the business may insist on annual audits to protect their investment in the business. In these cases the audit is a cost of using "outside" capital. But in many situations the outside sources of capital do not insist on audits. In these cases should a business have an audit?

Perhaps one or more of its employees are stealing money or other assets, accepting kickbacks, or manipulating sales prices for relatives or friends. The record of employee theft and dishonesty is not a good one, unfortunately. An audit may uncover employee theft and dishonesty, or deter potential theft and dishonesty. But this is *not* the main purpose of an audit of financial reports.

A business should not have an audit if, in fact, it wants a security check. The business should ask the CPA to come in and closely study and evaluate its internal controls to deter and detect employee theft and dishonesty. This sort of investigation may be very useful, but it is *not* an audit of the financial report, which is for a different purpose.

What Are the Limits of Audits? Do CPAs Look for Fraud? Will They Catch All Errors?

To get to the point directly, auditors do *not* catch everything. If top-level managers cleverly conceal their own dishonesty or illegal acts and lie to the auditors as part of the cover-up, it's unlikely the auditors will discover this sort of high-level fraud. The auditors may find other evidence of such fraud, but the chances are not good. There are many cases where management fraud has gone on several years before coming to light, and then usually not by audit discovery. In short, audits (of financial reports) cannot be relied on to uncover all high-level management dishonesty and illegal acts.

What about unintentional errors that may creep into the accounting recordkeeping process during the year? If there is a repetitive pattern of these errors, the auditors are likely to catch these errors. On the other hand, if the errors are few and random in occurrence, the auditor may not catch the errors unless the errors result in a material overstatement or understatement of the year-end balance in an asset or liability.

The auditor takes samples from each of the populations of different transactions that took place during the year. Each sample is not big, but it is selected very carefully and the items in the sample are examined very closely. So if the errors follow a pattern of repetition, there usually will be one or more errors in the sample. But the occasional, nonrepetitive type of error may not be included in the sample. However, the auditor does a lot of work to verify the ending balances of the assets, liabilities, and owners' equities. If an error has carried forward and affects the ending balance, there is a high chance that the auditor will catch it.

Last, what about employee theft and dishonesty? CPA auditors are very concerned about this. The auditor carefully studies and evaluates the company's internal accounting controls that are designed to deter and detect errors as well as intentional irregularities by employees. If controls are weak, more audit procedures are directed to the weak areas. Serious weaknesses are called to management's attention.

Nevertheless, collusion among two or more employees who work together in a conspiracy to cheat the business is difficult for the auditor to discover. Also, unrecorded transactions, such as skimming off the top of sales revenue, are difficult to discover. To the extent possible, a business is wise to employ other precautions such as rotation of duties among employees and, while employees take their vacations, assigning a replacement to do the work of the employee on vacation. A business should not rely on the audit alone. In fact, CPAs will (or should) tell managers to institute such controls.

Using a CPA to Review or Prepare Financial Statements Instead of Auditing Them

An audit may be too costly; the cost of the audit could be more than the interest on the loan to a smaller business. Bankers and other sources of loans to business understand this. Often lenders do not insist on an audit. Yet they prefer that a CPA at least "look over" the financial reports of companies they loan money to.

A CPA can perform certain limited procedures called a *review*. A review is *far less* than a full-scale audit. But a review does provide the CPA with a basis of information about the financial report. Based on the review, the CPA can state that he or she is not aware of any modifications (changes) that are needed to make the financial statements conform with generally accepted accounting principles. This is said in the final paragraph of the auditor's report. However, the CPA (reviewer) also warns the reader earlier in the report that a review is substantially less than an audit and that, accordingly, no opinion is being expressed on the financial report.

In short, based on a review the CPA does not give an affirmative opinion report; instead, the auditor gives a negative assurance ("no modifications are needed . . ."). This negative assurance is enough to satisfy the lender in many cases.

An audit or a review by a CPA is made of the financial statements prepared by the business itself. Many smaller companies, on the other hand, need the help of a CPA to prepare their financial statements in the first place. These companies don't have a professionally qualified accountant on their payroll. They use a CPA as a "part-time Controller" (chief accountant) to pull together their financial statements.

In this situation the CPA is said to *compile* the financial statements. No audit and no review is done; so, the CPA must disclaim any opinion on the financial report, and no negative assurance may be given either.

Other Services of CPAs

CPAs also offer tax services and management advisory (consulting) services to their clients. Many businesses cannot afford to hire a full-time accounting employee who is a specialist in income tax laws. The federal income tax law is so complex and changes so often that it takes a knowledgeable expert to keep a business in compliance with the law, and to take maximum advantage of all the options and provisions of the law. By specializing in taxes, a CPA can offer his or her services to many different businesses, none of whom could employ the CPA on a full-time basis.

CPAs also offer to consult on a variety of matters. They will advise a business on how to improve its internal controls, how to improve its data processing procedures, what type of computer system to use, what cost accounting methods are most appropriate, and so on.

20

MANIPULATING THE NUMBERS
—A LEGITIMATE GAME

The Name of the Game

Financial report audits by CPAs provide assurance that generally accepted accounting principles have been followed. (The CPA must point out any significant deviations, as Chapter 19 explains.) Basically, the CPA assures the creditors and stock investors who rely on financial reports that the business is playing fair in reporting its net income and financial condition. Playing fair means that the rules (generally accepted accounting principles) have been followed to measure sales revenue and expenses and thus profit, and asset values and liability amounts —the "numbers".

Like most nonaccountants, you probably assume that for each number there is one and only one rule. You probably think that once the facts of a company's transactions and operations have been identified and analyzed, there emerges one and only one set of numbers. Quite naturally you may suppose that the same facts lead to the same accounting methods to measure profit and financial condition. You're wrong.

Given the same facts, we know that different judges and juries reach different conclusions. Likewise in financial accounting. The same facts do not necessarily lead to the same accounting methods. Financial accounting would seem to be like measuring a person's weight, wouldn't it? But in fact, financial accounting also involves choosing the scale—one that weighs light or one that weighs heavy, or possibly one that weighs in between. In short, for many financial statement numbers there's not just one rule, but two rules or even three rules. The game can be played fairly by any one of the rules. Choices must be made from among *alternative* equally accepted accounting methods.

The conditions of each case do *not* dictate the method that has to be used. For example, in periods of rising costs, either a conservative "keep the profits down" cost of goods sold expense method may be used, or a more generous method may be used. And in periods of stable costs, either method may be selected. For another example, regardless of whether long-lived asset replacement costs are increasing or holding level, either a rapid (accelerated) or slower (straight-line) depreciation method may be used. The selection of the depreciation method does not depend on what's happening to replacement costs of the company's fixed assets.

Many deplore this "looseness" or "elasticity" of accounting methods. In theory, one accounting method would seem the

EXHIBIT J—THE RANGE OF ACCOUNTING METHODS

Unaccepatable Methods that Would Be Too Conservative	*Range of Acceptable Accounting Methods (choice of methods within this range are in conformity with generally accepted accounting principles)*		*Unaccepable Methods That Would Be Too Liberal*
– – – – – – – – – –	← – →		– – – – – – – – – –
Such unacceptable methods would include:	(Minimum Limit)	(Maximum Limit)	Such unacceptable methods would include:

← – – – – – – INCOME STATEMENT – – – – – – →

—Arbitrarily charging off to expense now the cost of inventory that will not be sold until later	—Annual profit is measured as low as possible; sales revenue is recorded at lowest possible amounts, and expenses are recorded at highest possible amounts.	—Annual profit is measured as high as possible; sales revenue is recorded at highest possible amounts, and expenses are recorded at lowest possible amounts.	—Not writing-off the cost of unsalable inventory
—Charging to expense now the cost of a major long-lived asset that will be used for several future years			—Depreciation of a long-lived asset over a much longer period than it will be useful to the business

← – – – – – – BALANCE SHEET – – – – – – →

—Recording expenses for vague and nonspecific contingency losses that probably will not happen	—Assets are recorded as low as possible because expenses are charged-out at highest amounts or at earliest time, and thus the assets involved contain the smallest cost residuals.	—Assets are recorded as high as possible because expenses are charged-out at lowest amounts or at latest time and thus the assets involved contain the largest cost residuals.	—Failure to recognize the impending loss from a lawsuit the business will lose, or other assessments the business will have to pay.
—Delaying the recording of sales that have been made in the ordinary course of business			—Recording sales before the sales are final, or failure to recognize the likelihood of large returns of products or large bad debts.
	—Certain liabilities are recorded at highest amounts because the expenses involving these liabilities are recorded at the largest amounts possible.	—Certain liabilities are recorded at lowest amounts because the expenses involving the liabilities are recorded at the lowest amounts possible.	

preferred or best method in particular cicumstances. In other words, specific conditions would seem to lead to one and only one accounting method. So if two different businesses were in the same set of circumstances, their accounting methods would be the same. But in fact, their accounting methods might be different.

The authoritative pronouncements on generally accepted accounting principles over the years have narrowed down the range of acceptable methods, to be sure. But within this range there are still choices to be made. For an illustration of this, see Exhibit J on page 109.

The chief executive has to make certain that the company's financial statements stay within the bounds of fairness, that is, that the accounting choices are those in the range of accepted methods. If the accounting methods are outside these limits, the financial statements will be false and misleading, and the manager will be liable for damages suffered by those debtholders and stockholders who relied on the statements. If for no other reason than this, the manager has to pay close attention to the choice of accounting methods used to prepare the company's financial statement numbers.

Once an accounting method is decided upon the business must, for all practical purposes, stick with the method consistently year to year. So, if a business chooses a conservative set of accounting methods, its financial statements will continue to be conservative for many years.

Last, it should be mentioned that the real, or ultimate driving force behind the accounting numbers is the profit making ability of management—making sales and controlling expenses. The choice of accounting methods makes a difference, to be sure, but only in a marginal sense, not in a fundamental sense.

Managers Should Manipulate the Numbers

Business managers may try to avoid getting involved in choosing accounting methods. But this is a mistake. First, there is the risk that the financial statements are not prepared according to generally accepted accounting principles in one or more respects. Using CPAs to audit the financial statements minimizes the risk of releasing misleading statements. However, even financial statements that have been audited by very respectable CPA firms have been found deficient; managers and CPAs have been found guilty in court trials, and they had had to pay large damages to debtholders and stockholders. Managers certainly have to keep aware of the consequences of reporting misleading financial statements. But there is a more important reason for managers getting involved in making accounting choices.

The business manager should decide which accounting methods best fit the general policies and philosophy of the business. In other words, the manager has to decide which "look" of the financial statements is in the best interests of the company. Putting it more crudely, the manager can and should manipulate the profit numbers, and the asset and liability numbers that are reported in the financial statements.

The point is this: the numbers have to be manipulated—if not by the managers, then by their accountants. By staying out of the decision making, the manager allows the accountant to do the manipulating. But the accountant may not be fully aware of all the policies of the company and the various pressures on the business. The manager may, given all the pressures and problems at the present time, need a rather "aggressive" set of financial statements, say to persuade the bank to make a loan or to convince a major customer of the financial ability of the company to carry through on a major deal or a long-term contract. But the accountant may choose conservative accounting methods instead.

The managers should select those accounting methods that best advance the interests of the business. The manager should ask whether the accounting methods of the business should be on the conservative end, in the middle, or on the liberal end of the range of generally accepted methods. These are not easy decisions. But the decisions are too important to leave to the accountant alone. And in the process of getting involved, the manager will certainly develop a much better understanding of financial statements, which helps in analyzing profit performance and financial position, and in "talking" the financial statements when borrowing money or when raising equity capital.

Advice for Creditors and Investors

If you're a creditor or an investor, you may be rather shocked by the advice just given business managers. You may think that financial statements should be based on accounting methods completely objective and tamper-proof. Advising managers to manipulate the numbers may seem against your interests. Of course, you probably do just this in filling out your income tax returns, don't you? And for good reasons, you would argue.

Like it or not, we live in a world of alternative accounting methods. Choices have to be made, and thus financial statements are flexible. The financial statements for each business come in a "small, medium, or large size," depending on which specific methods are used to account for the profit making activities of the business. The best you can do is to determine whether the business is being conservative or not so conservative in its financial statements, and then to make lending and investment decisions with this in mind.

The overall conservatism of the financial statements of a business depends on two accounting methods in particular—its cost of goods sold method and its depreciation method. Other accounting choices also affect financial statements. But the cost of goods sold and depreciation methods set the tone for most businesses.

The next two chapters discuss these two important accounting methods.

21

THE COST OF GOODS SOLD
CONUNDRUM

The Importance of This Accounting Decision: Introducing the Example

The cost of products sold to customers usually is a company's largest single expense, commonly being 60–70% of sales revenue. Gross profit and all the profit lines below gross profit are very sensitive to how the cost of goods (products) sold expense is measured. Clearly, managers have a high stake in how much profit is earned, so managers should understand how the biggest deduction against sales revenue is measured. As a matter of fact, the chief executive should make the accounting decision regarding which method shall be used by the business to measure its costs of goods sold expense.

There are three basic methods used widely to determine the cost of goods sold expense. All three methods have theoretical support, and all three methods are acceptable interpretations of the general accounting principle that cost of goods sold should be deducted against sales revenue in the same period to measure gross profit for the period.

A specific example is needed to demonstrate the accounting problem and to contrast the differences between the three accounting methods. Not only is the cost of goods sold expense for the period different by each method. The ending inventory cost resulting from each method is also different.

Assume that a company sold 4000 units of a particular product during the year. The company's inventory equals 13 weeks of its annual sales, or ¼ of annual sales (13 weeks ÷ 52 weeks = ¼). The company started the year with 1000 units of the product, which is the carry-forward from last year. During the year the company made four purchases of 1000 units each to replenish its stock of this product as sales were made during the year. So the company ended the year with 1000 units in inventory.

Purchase costs increased during the year. Exhibit K on page 115 shows the purchase cost information and also illustrates the essence of each of the three accounting methods that are explained next.

EXHIBIT K—COMPARISON OF COST OF GOODS SOLD EXPENSE ACCOUNTING METHODS

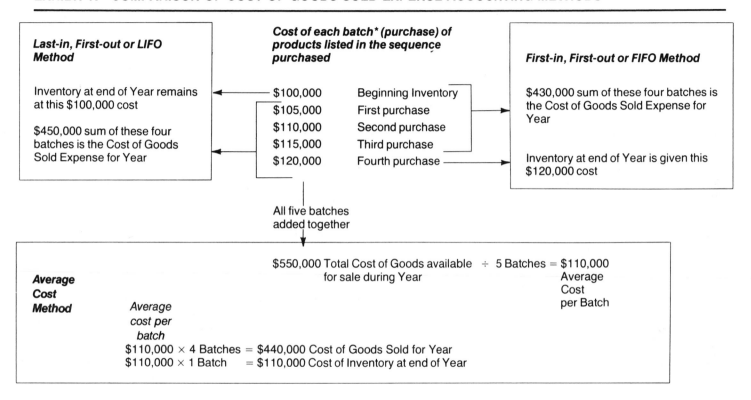

Last-in, First-out or LIFO Method

Inventory at end of Year remains at this $100,000 cost

$450,000 sum of these four batches is the Cost of Goods Sold Expense for Year

Cost of each batch* (purchase) of products listed in the sequence purchased

$100,000	Beginning Inventory
$105,000	First purchase
$110,000	Second purchase
$115,000	Third purchase
$120,000	Fourth purchase

First-in, First-out or FIFO Method

$430,000 sum of these four batches is the Cost of Goods Sold Expense for Year

Inventory at end of Year is given this $120,000 cost

All five batches added together

Average Cost Method

$550,000 Total Cost of Goods available for sale during Year ÷ 5 Batches = $110,000 Average Cost per Batch

Average cost per batch

$110,000 × 4 Batches = $440,000 Cost of Goods Sold for Year
$110,000 × 1 Batch = $110,000 Cost of Inventory at end of Year

* Each batch consists of 1000 units of product.

The Basics of LIFO, FIFO, and Average Cost Methods

In this example there are five equal size batches or groups, each being a separate purchase of 1000 units. Each batch has a different cost—this is the nub of the accounting problem. During the year 4000 units of the product were sold, and at year-end 1000 units are in inventory. Therefore, four batches should be charged to cost of goods sold expense for the year, and one batch should be the cost of ending inventory. But which batches to expense, and which batch to inventory?

The last-in, first-out, or LIFO method, selects the four batches that were purchased during the year and charges this $450,000 total cost to expense (see Exhibit K). The last-in, or most recent purchases are the first charged-out to expense. Purchase costs increased during the year, so LIFO maximizes the Cost of Goods Sold Expense. The beginning inventory batch, in this example the $100,000 cost of inventory at the start of the year, remains as the cost of the ending inventory at the close of the year. The actual products on hand at the end of the year are those bought most recently. Nevertheless, LIFO allows the cost of ending inventory to be the residual batch left over after selecting the more recent batches to charge to expense for the year. Thus the LIFO method allocates to ending inventory the "old" $100,000 cost.

The primary theory of the LIFO method is that products sold have to be replaced to continue in business, and that the most recent (i.e., the last-in) costs are the closest to the costs of replacing the products sold. When there is cost inflation (as in this example), LIFO maximizes the cost of goods sold expense and thus minimizes the profit reported in the Income Statement. To do this, however, inventory is reported at the lowest cost in the Balance Sheet.

The reverse of the LIFO method is the first-in, first-out, or FIFO method. The FIFO method selects the beginning inventory batch and the first, second, and third purchases during the year, and charges this $430,000 total cost to expense (see Exhibit K). The first batches in are the first batches to be charged-out to expense. The $120,000 cost batch, being the last purchase during the year, becomes the cost of the ending inventory.

The primary theory of FIFO is that the actual flow of products usually is a first-in, first-out sequence. When there is cost inflation during the year (as in this example), FIFO minimizes the cost of goods sold expense and thus maximizes the profit reported in the Income Statement. And inventory is reported at the highest cost in the Balance Sheet.

The Average Cost method pools all five batches into one total cost of $550,000 to get an average cost per batch of $110,000. Based on this average cost, $440,000 is allocated to expense for the year, and the ending inventory is allocated $110,000 (see Exhibit K).

The LIFO and FIFO methods are the co-favorites. The Average Cost method is a distant third in popularity. The Average Cost method could be used as the natural compromise, but as a practical matter, the decision usually comes down to a choice between LIFO and FIFO.

What Difference Does It Make?

In this example purchase costs increased 20% during the year, which is not unrealistic given the inflationary environment of business. LIFO results in $20,000 less reported gross profit compared with the FIFO method. In other words, LIFO gives a cost of goods sold expense that is $20,000 more than FIFO. Assume that total sales revenue from the 4000 units sold during the year was $645,000 based on gross profit equal to ⅓ of sales revenue, which is the experience of the company in this example. (The sales revenue amount is developed in more detail later in this chapter.) The $20,000 difference between LIFO and FIFO is about 3% of sales revenue.

A 3% difference may not seem like much. But remember that the $20,000 carries down and results in the same amount of difference in the profit before income tax. In the example used in previous chapters, the company's profit before income tax is about 7% of sales revenue. A 3% difference on the 7% base of profit before income tax means that the LIFO or FIFO choice has an enormous impact on reported profit: $3/_7$ more profit if FIFO is selected, or $3/_7$ less profit if LIFO is selected.

Assume that costs had increased only 10% during the year, instead of 20%, and assume that the company's pre-tax profit was in the 10–12% range, which is more typical for most businesses. Even in this more typical case, the LIFO versus FIFO impact on reported profit would be about ⅛, which is still a relatively large impact that managers, and creditors and investors as well, should not ignore.

And what about inventory? Ending inventory is reported at $100,000 cost by LIFO, compared to $120,000 cost by FIFO (see Exhibit K). LIFO causes the asset to be reported at ⅙ less cost than FIFO in the Balance sheet. This penalizes the current ratio, a key solvency ratio discussed in Chapter 23. The company's total current assets will look smaller compared with its total current liabilities.

In brief summary: during periods of rising costs, LIFO results in the lowest reported profit and the lowest reported inventory cost. Why, therefore, do companies use LIFO? One possible reason is conservatism. They want to err on the downside and not be accused of overstating profits or assets. Another possible reason for LIFO is to minimize profits that are subject to profit sharing plans for employees or second-level managers, or bonus plans based on profits. Keeping reported profits low keeps the profit shares or bonuses low. Another reason might be to "hide" profits during periods of labor problems or union contract bargaining. Also, a company may need to make the argument that it needs to earn more profit and thus has to raise its sales prices.

Or, the main reason may be to minimize *taxable income*. LIFO is allowed for federal and state income tax purposes. Consider the inventory example again. Compared with FIFO, the LIFO method reduces gross profit by $20,000, and thus taxable income is also $20,000 less. At a 50% tax rate, this reduces taxes on this year's profit by $10,000. So $10,000 less *cash* has to be paid out for income tax; cash flow is $10,000 higher.

The cash flow benefit is important for three main reasons. First, a business may be in a very tight cash situation and really need to hang on to every possible dollar it can. Second, the business probably can put the extra $10,000 to work and earn 10% or more per year on the money. Third, assuming that inflation will continue, a business might as well delay paying its taxes as long as possible and pay off in the cheaper dollars of the future.

LIFO Liquidation Gains:
A Special Feature of LIFO

Once a business selects LIFO, it must remain consistent with it over the entire life cycle of the product. LIFO is a long-term commitment. (This is true for all accounting methods in most cases, as mentioned before.)

Furthermore, the business manager should think ahead about what happens in the last year of the product's life cycle. In this last year there is a *LIFO liquidation profit* that causes a rather large "blip," or one-time gain caused by selling out of the inventory. Refer again to Exhibit K on page 115. Now assume we are at a time 5 years later, and this product was phased out during this last year. To simplify, assume that the company has kept its inventory at the same 1000 units level.

During the last year, assume that the average cost of each purchase is $220,000, due to inflation every year since the year used in the example. Normally the company would make four purchases during the year and the total cost of these four purchases is charged to cost of goods sold expense by the LIFO method. *But*, in the last year the company makes only three purchases and liquidates all its inventory of 1000 units to provide the rest of its sales. This "old batch" causes the problem.

The cost of the old batch that is charged to cost of goods sold expense is $100,000, not the current prevailing purchase cost of $220,000. So there is a one-time nonrecurring gain of $120,000 in gross profit! And, taxable income is also $120,000 higher as a result of the inventory liquidation.

All a business does by using LIFO is delay the reporting of a certain amount of profit, both in its annual Income Statements and its annual tax returns. Eventually, when the business reaches the end of the product's life cycle and liquidates its inventory, the profit that would have been recorded along the way by the FIFO method "catches up" with the business and has to be recorded.

Managers certainly should be aware of the eventual LIFO liquidation gain at the end of a product's life cycle. To go a step further on this point; the manager does not have to wait until the end of the life cycle. Instead, the manager could "force" this effect by deliberately allowing LIFO based inventory to fall below normal levels. Toward the end of the year the manager could hold off purchases, thus causing the ending inventory quantity to fall to abnormally low levels. Or, a severe business downturn, such as in the early 1980s, may force the business to drastically reduce its inventory levels and thus to dip into its old LIFO layers.

In short, the business has some potential profit in reserve, or "on the shelf," in the form of inventory carried on the LIFO cost basis. There is nothing to prohibit management manipulation of reported profit by the partial liquidation of LIFO costed inventory. The manager can do this without any objection from the CPA auditing the financial statements, although such LIFO liquidation gains have to be reported in a footnote to the company's financial statements (if material).

Should the LIFO or FIFO Choice Be Consistent with Sales Pricing Policy?

Assume that you're the manager who sets sales prices for the product in the example. Needless to say, many factors and pressures affect sales prices. But to simplify somewhat, assume that normally you base your sales price on the most recent purchase cost and you let all the units in this batch go out at this sales price until you exhaust the batch. When you start selling from the next batch, you change your sales price based on the new cost of the next batch. As mentioned earlier, your sales price is based on a 50% mark-up on cost, which means that gross profit is ⅓ of sales revenue. For example, if the purchase cost is $2.00, a $1.00 mark-up is added to get the $3.00 sales price.

Given these assumptions regarding sales pricing, your total sales revenue for the year is determined as follows (see Exhibit K for purchase costs):

Batch	Purchase Cost	50% Mark-Up	Sales Revenue
Beginning Inventory	$100,000 +	$50,000 =	$150,000
First Purchase	$105,000 +	$52,500 =	$157,500
Second Purchase	$110,000 +	$55,000 =	$165,000
Third Purchase	$115,000 +	$57,500 =	$172,500
Total Sales Revenue For the Year			$ 645,000

This schedule should make clear that you are following a first-in, first-out, or FIFO, sales price policy.

You should be very interested in the results that would be reported in your annual Income Statement by the LIFO and FIFO methods:

INCOME STATEMENT

	LIFO		FIFO	
	Amount	Percent	Amount	Percent
Sales Revenue	$645,000	100.0	$645,000	100.0
Cost of Goods Sold	450,000	69.8	430,000	66.7
Gross Profit	$195,000	30.2	$215,000	33.3

FIFO gives results consistent with your sales price policy: the cost of goods sold expense is exactly ⅔ (66.7%) of sales revenue, and gross profit is exactly ⅓ (33.3%) of sales revenue.

LIFO, on the other hand, reports that you are falling short of your gross profit goal. Managers, of course, rely on Income Statements for feedback on profit performance. The LIFO method suggests that you should raise prices because your gross profit is only 30.2% of sales revenue. The LIFO method may be used to determine Cost of Goods Sold Expense. But this does not mean that the company is able to set its sales prices on the LIFO basis.

LIFO sales prices would be based on the *next* purchase cost, i.e., the costs of replacing the units sold. In this example, the LIFO sales prices would be based on the last four purchases shown in Exhibit K ($105,000, $110,000, $115,000, and $120,000). This would require total sales revenue of $675,000, instead of $645,000, or $30,000 more sales revenue.

But could the higher prices have been charged to customers? Normally competitive pressures keep sales prices down, or delay the increase of sales prices. In short, a company's sales price policy may be "forced" by competitive pressures to stay on a FIFO basis. If costs of goods sold expense is on a LIFO basis, reported gross profit will be somewhat misleading. Managers definitely should keep this in mind when analyzing the gross profit performance numbers reported in their Income Statements. Likewise, creditors and investors should allow for this in evaluating a company's profit performance.

22

ACCELERATED OR STRAIGHT-LINE DEPRECIATION?

Deciding Whether to Put Certain Costs in Long-Lived Assets as Capitalized Costs

When acquiring most long-lived assets, there are certain costs that could be put in asset accounts, but don't have to be. In pure theory these costs should be "capitalized," which means that the costs should be recorded in asset accounts and included in their total cost. As a practical matter, however, these costs don't have to be capitalized. CPA auditors and the IRS do not object if the costs "bypass" the asset accounts.

For example, assume a business has just bought a new delivery truck. The purchase cost paid to the truck dealer has to be capitalized, including the sales tax paid to the dealer. There usually are other incidental costs, however. The truck may be painted with the company's name, address, and logo. The business may put special racks or fittings in the truck. In theory, these additional costs should be capitalized and included in the asset account. But the costs are not directly a part of the purchase cost; the costs are, as a practical matter, detachable from the purchase cost.

Many long-lived asset acquisitions involve such additional detachable costs. New buildings certainly do. Beyond the basic contract price of a building the company usually has many additional moving-in and preparation costs. Likewise, in addition to the purchase cost of a new machine or a new piece of equipment, a business typically has installation costs.

Also, almost all businesses buy many tools such as hammers, power saws, drills, floor cleaning machines, dollies, and so on. In theory the cost of these relatively low cost tools should be capitalized if they will be used more than 1 year.

For convenience the additional detachable costs associated with the acquisition of long-lived assets and the cost of small tools and like items will be called *grey area costs* in the following discussion.

Say a business has just purchased a new long-lived asset and has paid $50,000 cash for the asset. Shortly following the purchase the business incurs $5000 additional grey area costs.

The $50,000 has to be capitalized, and accordingly is put in an asset account. If not, the CPA auditors would certainly object, and the IRS could accuse the business of tax evasion. In other words, charging-off the $50,000 to expense immediately is clearly in violation of generally accepted accounting principles (GAAP) and income tax laws. The $50,000 has to be

EXHIBIT L—COMPARISON OF CAPITALIZING VERSUS NOT CAPITALIZING GREY AREA LONG-LIVED ASSET COSTS

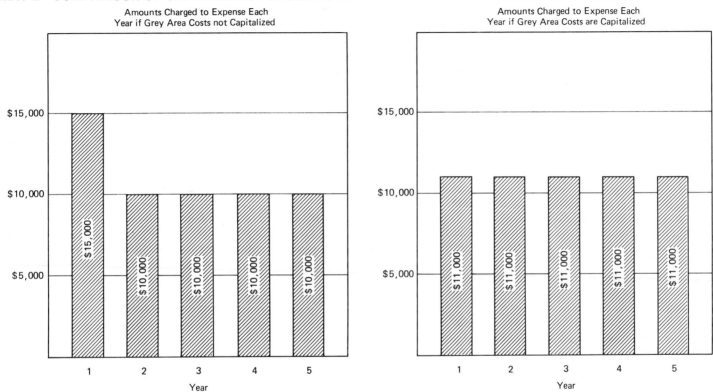

allocated over the future years of use expected from the asset. Chapter 10 explains the basic theory of depreciation accounting.

On the other hand, the business manager could decide to allow the $5000 of grey area costs to fall into expense this period. Instead of capitalizing the additional $5000, all this amount could be charged to expense this period. This penalizes this year's profits, but relieves the future years of this much additional depreciation expense.

Assume that the asset is depreciated over 5 years. Also

assume that an equal amount of depreciation is charged to each year (just to simplify the example here). The impact on expenses for each year from the decision to capitalize versus not to capitalize the gray area costs is shown in Exhibit L on page 127.

Not to capitalize the grey area costs is very conservative. The first year's expenses absorb an extra $5000, and the asset is reported at the lower cost value in the Balance Sheet. On the other hand, it must be remembered that in making this choice the company escapes a certain amount of depreciation expense in each future year. There is a "robbing Peter to pay Paul" effect. In the example above, year 1 is "robbed" by absorbing $4000 additional expense, but years 2, 3, 4, and 5 are "paid" $1000 additional profit. On the other hand, if the grey area costs are capitalized, each year is treated equally.

The main reason for not capitalizing grey area costs is to minimize taxable income in the first year (the year of acquiring long-lived assets). In the first year the amount paid out for taxes is lowered, and the company has the use of the tax saving until it has to be paid back in the future years. (Don't forget that taxable income in each of the future years is higher.) The cash flow advantage in the first year is very persuasive. This "free loan"

from the government, plus the more conservative look of their financial statements, cause many managers not to capitalize grey area costs.

Last, the policy of not capitalizing grey area costs and charging them entirely to expense in the first year provides business managers another way to manipulate reported profit. The timing of many of these expenditures is somewhat discretionary. Small tools can be replaced at the end of this year, or replacement can be delayed to the start of next year. Thus the expense can be held-off until next year. Also, the acquisition of several assets can be delayed and "slipped-over" to the following year. So the associated grey area costs would not be recorded as expense until next year. In reverse, the purchase of small tools and fixed assets can be speeded up, and thus the grey costs would be recorded as expense this year instead of next year.

On the other hand, it can be argued that without any deliberate management manipulation the amount of grey area costs tends to be more or less the same year to year. So, there is a more or less "wash-out" effect every year, and the net difference would be negligible. Indeed, for a mature business this may not be far off the mark.

Deciding on Useful Life Estimates and Depreciation Methods

A building may stand 60–100 years. Yet the IRS allows a 15-year depreciation life for tax purposes. An office desk may last 20 years, yet the IRS allows a 5-year life for this type of asset.

In short, the federal income tax permits long-lived assets to be depreciated over life spans that are too short, compared with the actual useful lives of the assets. This is a deliberate policy of the federal government, to encourage investment and to allow business to recover capital invested in assets as quickly as possible.

It's fair to say that the federal tax laws regarding depreciation lives have removed any attempt to be realistic in estimating the useful life spans of long-lived assets. In brief, the shortest allowed lives are adopted by the large majority of businesses. These "short lives" are found in the Accelerated Cost Recovery System (ACRS) now a part of our federal income tax laws. In fact, there's hardly any point arguing for more realistic (longer) life estimates.

All financial statement users should keep in mind that long-lived assets are depreciated too fast—not in the actual wearing out or economic sense, mind you, but in the accounting/recordkeeping sense. The reported values of these assets in Balance Sheets are very conservative for this reason. This, plus the rapid pace of inflation, means that after a few years the total book value of a company's long-lived assets is far below the total current replacement cost of the assets. (Larger publicly owned corporations are required to disclose estimated current replacement costs of their long-lived assets, in supplementary footnotes to their financial reports.)

Basically, a business has two alternatives regarding depreciation of its long-lived assets:

1. Adopt the ACRS schedule, which uses very short lives for the assets, and which also has a little bit of a front-end "hump" in the spreading of the depreciation year by year; or,

2. Adopt more realistic (longer) useful life estimates for the assets and spread the annual depreciation over the useful life of each asset according to the *straight-line* method. The straight-line method simply means allocating an equal amount of depreciation to each (full) year of use of the asset.

EXHIBIT M—COMPARISON OF ACRS (ACCELERATED) AND STRAIGHT-LINE (LONGER LIFE) DEPRECIATION METHODS—MACHINE COST = $120,000

ANNUAL DEPRECIATION AMOUNT

	ACRS Method	Straight-Line Method
Year 1	$ 18,000	$ 5,000 (only one-half year allowed)
Year 2	26,400	10,000
Year 3	25,200	10,000
Year 4	25,200	10,000
Year 5	25,200	10,000
Year 6	—0—	10,000
Year 7	—0—	10,000
Year 8	—0—	10,000
Year 9	—0—	10,000
Year 10	—0—	10,000
Year 11	—0—	10,000
Year 12	—0—	10,000
Year 13	—0—	5,000 (final one-half year)
Total	$120,000	$120,000

Note: To simplify, the asset's total cost of $120,000 is depreciated in the above comparison. However, if the full investment tax credit is taken, then a small percent of the asset's cost may not be depreciated, and in theory the asset's estimated salvage value at disposal should not be depreciated. Last, assets placed in service prior to 1981 are subject to different useful lives for tax purposes as well as different methods of accelerated allocation over their useful lives.

For example, assume a business buys a new machine. The ACRS method allows this asset to be depreciated over 5 years. Alternatively, the business may use a 12 year useful life estimate, which we'll assume to be realistic for this particular kind of machine. Exhibit M shows the difference in depreciation year by year, assuming the cost of the machine is $120,000.

Although accelerated (ACRS) depreciation has obvious income tax advantages, there are certain disadvantages. For one thing, the book (reported) values of long-lived assets are lower. Some borrowing is done on the basis of these assets; mortgages or other liens may be given on the assets, or lenders may consider book values in their decisions. The lower book values of its long-lived assets may lower the debt capacity of a business by using accelerated depreciation.

One final point: managers and investors are very interested in the growth (or decline) of profit year to year. Ideally, a profit increase this year over last year should be due to "real" causes such as better profit margins on sales, operating efficiency improvements, higher volumes, etc. Spurious increases in reported profit are misleading to managers and investors. Profit trends are difficult to track reliably if there are accounting "drop-offs" in annual depreciation expense, such as shown in Exhibit M after year five by the ACRS method. The straight-line method has the advantage of keeping the depreciation expense constant year to year (on the same assets).

23

RATIOS FOR CREDITORS
AND INVESTORS

When deciding whether to make or renew loans to businesses, bankers and other lenders direct their attention to particular financial statement ratios. Credit rating agencies, such as Dun & Bradstreet, compile financial statement ratios on thousands of businesses. The ratios provide a statistical profile of a business, for assessing its credit worthiness and the risk in extending credit to the business. If a company's ratios are weak, securing loans and trade credit becomes difficult.

Stock investors also focus on particular financial statement ratios. They are first concerned about whether the business will be able to pay its debts when they come due, as well as the overall liability situation of the business. Maintaining solvency (debt-paying ability) is essential for continuing operations, of course. Therefore, investors are interested in the same ratios as those looked at by the creditors.

But investors have the strongest interest in the earnings performance of the business. They use certain key ratios to evaluate its profit track record.

This chapter briefly explains the basic financial statement ratios used by creditors and investors. These "numbers" de-

EXHIBIT N—THE COMPANY'S FINANCIAL STATEMENTS FOR ITS FIRST YEAR OF BUSINESS (MODIFIED SLIGHTLY TO SHOW TOTAL LIABILITIES)

BALANCE SHEET AT END OF YEAR

Current Assets			Current Liabilities		
Cash		$ 162,000	Accounts Payable		$ 270,000
Accounts Receivable		486,000	Accrued Expenses		117,000
Inventory		702,000	Income Tax Payable		30,000
Prepaid Expenses		90,000	Notes Payable		220,000
Total Current Assets		$1,440,000	Total Current Liabilities		$ 637,000
			Long-Term Notes Payable, at 10.0%		300,000
Property, Plant, & Equipment			Total Liabilities		$ 937,000
Machinery, Equipment, Furniture, and Fixtures	$464,000		**Stockholders' Equity:**		
Accumulated Depreciation	116,000		Paid-In Capital (for which stock shares are issued)	$701,000	
Undepreciated Cost		348,000	Retained Earnings	150,000	
Total Assets		$1,788,000	Total		851,000
			Total Liabilities and Stockholders' Equity		$1,788,000

termine the borrowing capacity of the business. These ratios are the basic "scores" by which managers are judged by the suppliers of capital to the business.

Managers are investors too; most managers have a capital investment in their business—as the sole proprietor, as a partner, or as a stockholder. As an investor, managers should know which ratios to use in evaluating their investments.

The financial statements of the same company analyzed in previous chapters serve as the example in this chapter again. For convenience the company's Balance Sheet at the end of its first year of business and its Income Statement for the year are reproduced here—see Exhibit N, which we'll refer to often in this chapter.

Notice that the Cash Flow Statement for the year is not repeated. None of the ratios discussed in this chapter involve this statement, which may come as a surprise to you. Why not? Two reasons seem to explain this. First, the statement is designed to read as a whole and is limited to the sources and uses of cash during the year. Cash flow is vital, but not the complete story about the business. Second, traditionally the Cash Flow Statement has not been included in external financial reports, so creditors and investors did not have this information readily available.

INCOME STATEMENT FOR YEAR

Sales Revenue		$4,212,000
Cost of Goods Sold		2,808,000
Gross Profit		$1,404,000
Operating Expenses	$936,000	
Depreciation Expense	116,000	1,052,000
Operating Earnings		$ 352,000
Interest Expense		52,000
Earnings before Tax		$ 300,000
Income Tax Expense		150,000
Net Income		$ 150,000

Debt-Paying Ability (Solvency) Ratios

Always a key question is whether a business will be able to pay its liabilities when they come due. Failure to pay its debts on time damages the credit rating of the business, of course, and may jeopardize its very existence if the unpaid creditors take legal action to enforce collection. The sharp rise in business failures, including the bankruptcies of many well known corporations during the recession of the early 1980s, underscores the importance of keeping a close watch on the debt paying ability of a business.

The Current Ratio: The Basic Test of Short-Term Solvency

One "classic" and widely used ratio to test the short-term debtpaying ability of a company is its *current ratio*, which is the company's total current assets divided by its total current liabilities. From the data in Exhibit N, the current ratio for the company is computed as follows:

$$\text{Current Ratio} = \frac{\text{Total Current Assets}}{\text{Total Current Liabilities}} = \frac{\$1,440,000}{\$637,000} = 2.26$$

The current ratio may be expressed as 2.26 to 1.00, but hardly ever as a percent (226%).

The general rule of thumb is that the current ratio should be 2 to 1 or higher. Most businesses find that a minimum 2 to 1 current ratio is applied by their creditors. In other words, short-term creditors generally limit the credit extended a business to ½ or less of the company's short-term assets. Given this credit limit, a company's current assets will be twice or more its current liabilities.

Why do short-term creditors put such a limit on a business? One reason is to provide a safety cushion. A current ratio of 2 to 1 means there is $2 of cash or assets that will be converted into cash during the near future available to pay each dollar of current liabilities (which come due in the near future). Each dollar of short-term debt is "backed-up" with two dollars of present cash or future near-term cash inflow. The "extra" dollar of current assets provides a nice margin of safety.

Theoretically, a company could remain solvent with a 1 to 1 current ratio. The three noninterest bearing liabilities—Accounts Payable, Accrued Expenses, and Income Tax Payable—supply total credit equal to, say, about ⅓ of total current assets. With this base of current liabilities, the company could conceivably convince bankers or other lenders to make short-term loans for the other ⅔ of current assets. But this would leave no safety margin for the lenders. Few, if any, short-term lenders would go this far out on a limb.

After all, creditors are not owners—they don't share in the net income earned by the business. The income on their loans is limited to the interest rates they charge. As a creditor they quite properly minimize their loan risks; as limited-income investors they must.

In short, suppliers of short-term loans to business decide what the minimum current ratio shall be, and seldom do they allow it to drop below 2 to 1.

However, the 2 to 1 minimum is only a rule of thumb; there are exceptions. Some companies such as car dealers can borrow almost 100% on their inventories, so their current liabilities are more than ½ their current assets. Before accepting the 2 for 1 ratio for a business, it is a good idea to check the *average* current ratio for companies in the industry. For example, Dun & Bradstreet publishes the current ratio for a large number of industries. Motor vehicle dealers, as just mentioned, traditionally have carried on business with a 1.5 to 1.0 current ratio.

The Acid Test Ratio (or Quick Ratio)

Inventory is many weeks away from conversion into cash. Products are held 2, 3, or 4 months before sale. If the sale is made on credit, which is normal, there's another waiting period before the receivables are collected. In short, inventory is not nearly as liquid as Accounts Receivable; it takes a lot longer to convert Inventory into cash.

The *acid test ratio* excludes Inventory (and Prepaid Expenses

also). The total of Cash, Marketable Securities (if any), and Accounts Receivable is divided by total current liabilities to compute the acid test ratio. It is also called the *quick ratio* because only cash and assets quickly convertible into cash are included in the ratio. In this example the company's acid test ratio is computed as follows:

$$\text{Acid Test Ratio} = \frac{\text{Cash} + \text{Accounts Receivable}}{\text{Total Current Liabilities}}$$

$$= \frac{\$162,000 + \$486,000}{\$637,000} = 1.02$$

The rule of thumb is that the acid test ratio should be 1 to 1 or higher, although you find many more exceptions to this rule of thumb than the 2 to 1 current ratio.

Debt to Equity Ratio

Some debt is good, but too much debt is dangerous. The Debt to Equity ratio is an indicator whether a company is using debt to its advantage, or perhaps going too far and is overburdened with debt.

For the company in this example (Exhibit N), the debt to equity ratio is computed as follows:

$$\frac{\text{Debt/Equity}}{\text{Ratio}} = \frac{\text{Total Liabilities}}{\text{Total Stockholders' Equity}} = \frac{\$937,000}{\$851,000} = 1.10$$

In brief, the company is using $1.10 of liabilities for every $1.00 of owners' (stockholders') equity in the business. Notice that *all* liabilities (noninterest as well as interest bearing, and both short-term and long-term) are included, and *all* stockholders' equity (paid-in capital plus retained earnings) is included in the debt to equity ratio.

Most businesses stay below a 1 to 1 debt to equity ratio, because they don't want to take on so much debt or because they can't convince creditors to loan them more than one-half of their assets. However, some industries are exceptions to this rule of thumb, and traditionally have had debt to equity ratios higher than 1 to 1.

Return on Investment Ratios: How Financial Leverage Helps (Usually)

Stock investors take the risk of whether the business can earn a profit and sustain its profit performance over the years. The value of their stock depends first and foremost on the profit making record and potential of the business.

The basic test of a company's profit performance for its stockholders is not simply how much profit it earns, but rather how much profit is earned relative to how much stockholders' equity (capital) is being used to earn that profit. $100,000 annual net income relative to $250,000 stockholders' capital base is very good. $100,000 annual net income relative to $2,500,000 stockholders' capital base is very poor.

Dividing annual net income by total stockholders' equity gives the *return on equity* (ROE) ratio; for this company it is computed as follows:

$$\text{Return on Equity} = \frac{\text{Net Income}}{\text{Total Stockholders' Equity}} = \frac{\$150,000}{\$851,000} = 17.63\%$$

By most standards a 17.63% ROE would be judged pretty good. But, again, the ROE should be compared with industry wide averages for the current year to get a true reading.

ROE is the "bottom-line" return on investment (ROI) ratio for stockholders. Bottom-line profit (net income) is divided by the stockholders' equity in the business. Other ROI ratios are also useful in analyzing a company's profit performance.

Another very important ROI ratio for profit analysis is the *return on assets* (ROA) ratio. The before-tax ROA ratio is Operating Earnings (before interest and income tax) divided by Total Assets; for this company it is computed as follows:

$$\text{Before-Tax Return on Assets} = \frac{\text{Operating Earnings Before Interest and Income Tax}}{\text{Total Assets}}$$

$$= \frac{\$352,000}{\$1,788,000} = 19.69\%$$

The pre-tax ROA ratio tells us that the company earned more than 19¢ profit before interest and income tax on each dollar of assets used in the business.

The pre-tax ROA is compared with the annual interest rate on borrowed funds. In this example the company's annual interest rate on its short-term and long-term debt is 10.00%.

The company can earn 19.69% on the money borrowed. So there is a favorable "spread" of 9.69% between the two. This difference between the two rates is the nub of *financial leverage*. Financial leverage means using debt capital on which a business can earn a higher pre-tax ROA than the annual interest rate paid on the debt.

The total benefit from financial leverage can be computed fairly simply for a business. In this example the company has interest-bearing debt, as well as current liabilities on which no interest is paid. (This is true for almost all businesses, of course.) In total, all its liabilities supply $937,000 of the company's total assets (see Exhibit N on page 132).

The total cost for the use of this capital is the $52,000 interest expense for the year. Thus the company makes a sizable financial leverage gain on its liabilities, which is computed as follows:

Financial Leverage Gain for the Year

$937,000 × 19.69% = $184,465   (Operating earnings before
(Total Liabilities) (Pre-Tax ROA)   interest and income tax
                                        that is earned on the
                                        capital supplied by
                                        liabilities)

−52,000   (Interest expense)

$132,465   (Financial leverage
               gain for year)

Financial leverage provided over $132,000 of the $300,000 earnings before income tax for the year, or about 44%!

In a poor year a company's pre-tax ROA may be less than its annual interest rate. In this situation financial leverage (on borrowed funds) works against the company. The high interest rates of the early 1980s combined with the severe slippage in pre-tax ROA suffered by many businesses during this recessionary period provide ample proof of this point. The use of debt only aggravated an already bad situation for many corporations. Financial leverage cuts both ways, it should be remembered.

Price/Earnings (P/E) Ratio

The stock shares of more than ten thousand corporations are traded in public markets such as the New York Stock Exchange. The day to day market value of these shares receives a great deal of attention, to say the least. Market value, more than anything else, depends on the earnings ability of the corporation. Therefore, market value is compared to net income (earnings after interest and income tax, or the final, bottom line earnings of the corporation).

Because market value is per share, net income (earnings) has to be put on a per share basis. The basic idea of computing *Earnings per Share (EPS)* can be put as follows:

$$\text{Earnings per Share (EPS)} = \frac{\text{Net Income for Year}}{\text{Total Number of Stock Shares Participating in Net Income}}$$

EPS is not simple to compute, despite the relative simplicity of the concept. Public corporations use fairly complicated stock structures. They may issue preferred stock shares in addition to common stock shares. Their debt (and preferred stock) securities may be convertible into their common stock shares. Many other conditions affect the computation of the EPS.

In any case, once EPS is computed it is compared with the market price of the stock. The *Price/Earnings (P/E) ratio* is computed:

$$\text{Price/Earnings (P/E) Ratio} = \frac{\text{Current Market Price}}{\text{Earnings per Share}}$$

Suppose the stock shares were trading at $24.00 per share, and the corporation's EPS for the most recent year is $3.00. Thus its P/E ratio is 8.00. Like all the other ratios discussed in this chapter, the P/E ratio has to be compared against industry wide and market wide averages to tell if it's too high or too low. Much depends on the how stock investors forecast the future earnings prospects of the corporation.

The P/E ratio is so important that the *Wall Street Journal* includes it with other market trading information for all common stock shares reported in the New York Stock Exchange

(NYSE)—Composite Transactions as well as the American Stock Exchange (Amex)—Composite Transactions.

The P/E ratio does not apply to private corporations, whose stock shares are not traded. The stock owners and managers of these companies judge profit (earnings) performance mainly by Return on Equity (ROE) and other return on investment ratios. One of their main concerns is how to maintain and improve ROE.

Return on Equity: Final Comments

How can a business improve a poor ROE, or maintain a good ROE? Three factors are key:

1. Financial leverage—keep the debt to equity ratio at the optimum level.

2. Sales revenue on assets—keep the sales to assets ratio as high as possible.

3. Control expenses—keep the expense to sales ratio as low as possible.

In brief, use debt to best advantage, make the best sales revenue use of assets, and keep expenses as low as possible. Each of these three key factors is discussed in turn.

The company in this example is already at a debt to equity ratio of 1.10 (see page 135). As a practical matter the company probably couldn't increase this ratio very much. So not much improvement in its ROE can be made here.

Profit derives from sales. The higher the sales revenue from a particular set (given mix) of assets the better, unless the company sells at a loss. In this case the company's annual sales revenue is $4,212,000 compared with $1,788,000 total assets (see Exhibit N). Sales are more than two times assets; this key relationship is measured in the *Asset Turnover Ratio*, which is computed as follows:

$$\text{Asset Turnover Ratio} = \frac{\text{Sales Revenue}}{\text{Total Assets}} = \frac{\$4,212,000}{\$1,788,000} = 2.36$$

If the company could squeeze out more sales from the same assets, its profit and thus its ROE should increase. The additional sales revenue should normally yield additional profit. Put in reverse, a decrease in the Asset Turnover Ratio will decrease the ROE.

Last, profit can be improved by reducing the ratio of expenses to sales revenue. Certainly every business should be cost conscious and continuously be on a program of cost containment and reduction. Its managers should ruthlessly examine every dollar of expense. The Internal Revenue Service, of all people, probably has the best approach. The IRS demands two tests for any expense to be deductible—the expense must be *necessary* and must be *reasonable* in amount. It's hard to think of better guidelines for business managers.

24

LET'S SEE
WHAT YOU'VE LEARNED

This last chapter has a dual purpose: to provide a concise summary so you can quickly review the main points discussed in the book, and, second, to provide a means to test your understanding of financial statements. A question-and-answer format is used. TRY TO ANSWER EACH QUESTION BEFORE READING THE ANSWER TO THE QUESTION.

A new set of financial statements is used for the example in this chapter (see Exhibit O on page 145). The statements are for the company's first 2 years of business. The Balance Sheet at each year-end and the Income Statement for each year are presented in comparative format. But Cash Flow Statements are *not* given for either year.

One purpose of this chapter is to test your ability to derive cash flow information from the other two financial statements. You will be asked to take information directly from the Balance Sheets and Income Statements to analyze cash flows each year. In Exhibit O notice that the Balance Sheets and Income Statements are shown in their standard conventional formats.

A reminder: answer each question *before* reading the answer/discussion. Only in this way can you test your understanding of financial statements and identify which topics you should study again. Please note that the *concise answer* appears in italics, and as necessary, is accompanied by supporting discussion.

Question 1—Where did the company get its money to start business? What were its main sources of capital in Year One? What did the company do with the capital?

Answer—The stockholders invested $1.2 million in the business—see the amount in the Paid-In Capital account in the Stockholders'

Equity section of the Balance Sheet at the end of Year One, Exhibit O. *Also, the company borrowed $160,000 on short-term notes and another $100,000 on long-term notes* (see the amounts in these two liability accounts in the Balance Sheet at the end of Year One.) Year One was the first year of business; so the ending balances had to be from transactions during the year. All the accounts started the year with zero balances (amounts).

The stockholders put their money in the business at the start of the business, probably all at once, to get the company going. The $1.2 million invested by stockholders provided the base of equity (ownership) capital on which the company can borrow.

Together the equity and two debt sources provided $1,460,000 total capital, which was used to purchase long-lived assets and inventory, to prepay some expenses, to allow the company to give credit to its customers and wait for payment until later, and to provide a cash balance. All these assets are reported in the company's Balance Sheet. In the order just mentioned, see in Exhibit O Property, Plant, & Equipment at $896,000 original cost, Inventory at $572,000 cost, Prepaid Expenses at $84,000 cost, Accounts Receivable at the $330,000 amount of uncollected sales revenue, and the $196,000 Cash balance.

Question 2—Are there are any other items in the Balance Sheet at the end of Year One that you didn't mention in your answer to Question 1? If so, how do you think they got there?

Answer—Yes, there are three current liabilities not mentioned so far, and also there's the Retained Earnings account in the Stockholders' Equity section.

The largest part of the $190,400 owed on Accounts Payable is the result of inventory purchases made on credit; part of the stock of goods

EXHIBIT O—COMPARATIVE BALANCE SHEETS AND INCOME STATEMENTS

BALANCE SHEETS AT END OF EACH YEAR

	Year One	Year Two		Year One	Year Two
Current Assets			**Current Liabilities**		
Cash	$ 196,000	$ 482,000	Accounts Payable	$ 190,400	$ 340,200
Accounts Receivable	330,000	616,000	Accrued Expenses	64,000	82,000
Inventory	572,000	720,000	Income Tax Payable	27,000	47,000
Prepaid Expenses	84,000	70,000	Notes Payable	160,000	300,000
Total Current Assets	$1,182,000	$1,888,000	Total Current Liabilities	$ 441,400	$ 769,200
Property, Plant, & Equipment			**Long-Term Notes Payable, at 10.0%**	$ 100,000	$ 200,000
Machinery, Equipment, Furniture, and Fixtures	$ 896,000	$ 952,000	**Stockholders' Equity**		
Accumulated Depreciation	179,200	369,600	Paid-In Capital	$1,200,000	$1,200,000
			Retained Earnings	157,400	301,200
Undepreciated Cost	$ 716,800	$ 582,400	Total	$1,357,400	$1,501,200
Total Assets	$1,898,800	$2,470,400	Total Liabilities and S/Hs' Equity	$1,898,800	$2,470,400

INCOME STATEMENTS FOR EACH YEAR

	Year One		Year Two	
Sales Revenue		$3,432,000		$4,576,000
Cost of Goods Sold		2,288,000		3,120,000
Gross Profit		$1,144,000		$1,456,000
Operating Expenses	$624,000		$728,000	
Depreciation Expense	179,200	803,200	190,400	918,400
Operating Earnings		$ 340,800		$ 537,600
Interest Expense		26,000		50,000
Earnings before Tax		$ 314,800		$ 487,600
Income Tax Expense		157,400		243,800
Net Income		$ 157,400		$ 243,800

held by the company at year-end had not been paid for at the end of the year, and this amount is included in Accounts Payable. The remainder of the amount in the liability account is from expenses recorded in Year One that had not been paid by the end of the year. All of the $64,000 Accrued Expenses liability at the end of Year One is from certain expenses properly recorded in the year, but which were unpaid at the end of the year.

In short, inventory purchases made late in the year and several of the expenses recorded late in the year were not yet paid at the end of the year, and these are reflected either in the Accounts Payable or the Accrued Expenses account.

Likewise, the $27,000 Income Tax Payable ending balance is the amount of the company's total income tax expense for the year that was unpaid at the end of Year One.

Retained Earnings is *not* an asset account; it's a stockholders' equity account. In other words, Retained Earnings does *not* identify an asset. Like Paid-In Capital, *Retained Earnings is a source of assets account. This account keeps track of how much of a company's total assets has resulted from net income earned and retained (not distributed to its owners).*

To review briefly, there are three sources of assets: (1) liabilities, (2) investment of capital by stockholders, and (3) retention of profit. The different assets owned by a business *and* the different sources of its assets are accounted for, to report the financial condition of the business. There are accounts for each separate liability, the account for invested capital, and, last, the account for net income retained in the business.

Question 3—Did the company distribute any of its net income earned in Year One to its stockholders? In other words, did the company pay any dividends out of its bottom-line earnings earned in Year One? If so, how much?

Answer—From its Income Statement we see that the company earned $157,400 net income in Year One. This increased Retained Earnings. Dividends cause decreases in the account. From its Balance Sheet at the end of Year One we see that Retained Earnings has a balance of $157,400, the full amount of net income for the year. *No dividends were paid during the year; there were no decreases in Retained Earnings during the year.*

Question 4—While we're on the topic, did the company pay any dividends in Year Two? If so, how much?

Answer—Compare the balance in Retained Earnings at the end of Year Two with its balance at the end of Year One: $301,200 − $157,400 = $143,800 increase during Year Two. The company earned $243,800 net income in Year Two (see its Income Statement for the year, Exhibit O). But Retained Earnings increased only $143,800 from the end of Year One to the end of Year Two.

So, during the year there must have been a decrease of $100,000, offsetting the $243,800 net income increase to give the net increase in Retained Earnings of $143,800 during Year Two. *Dividends were $100,000 during Year Two.* The company earned $243,800 net income and paid dividends of $100,000, giving a net increase of $143,800 in Retained Earnings during Year Two.

Question 5—The company did not dispose of any long-lived assets during the first two years of business. What is the cost of these assets purchased each year? Is the Accumulated Depreciation balance at the end of each year consistent with the depreciation expense recorded each year?

Answer—In the Balance Sheet a company's depreciable assets are reported in *two* accounts, and it's very important to understand each account. The cost of the assets bought or constructed by a company is reported in one account. The portion of the cost that has been recorded to depreciation expense in the year just ended and in all previous years is reported in a second account called Accumulated Depreciation.

Year by year the Accumulated Depreciation account increases as depreciation expense is recorded on the assets. Cost minus accumulated depreciation gives the *book value* of the assets. Book value, in other words, is the undepreciated cost, that is, that part of the cost that has not yet been charged-off to depreciation expense. Book value is the amount included in the company's total assets.

In this example the company's Balance Sheet (Exhibit O) reports $896,000 cost of Machinery, Equipment, Furniture, and Fixtures at the end of Year One. Year One is the company's first year of business, so *$896,000 is the cost of these assets acquired during the first year.*

As stated in the question, there were no disposals of any assets during Year Two. So there were no decreases in the Machinery, Equipment, Furniture, and Fixtures account during the year from disposals. At the end of Year Two this account has a balance of $952,000 (see Exhibit O again). This amount is $56,000 higher than the balance at the end of Year One: $952,000 balance at end of Year Two − $896,000 balance at end of Year One = $56,000 increase during Year Two. *Thus the cost of assets bought during the second year must have been $56,000.*

From the Income Statement (Exhibit O) we see that $179,200 was recorded as Depreciation Expense in Year One. No assets were disposed of during the year, so the Accumulated Depreciation account should have a balance of $179,200 at the end of Year One. Indeed it does (see Exhibit O).

No assets were disposed of in Year Two, as mentioned before. Thus there were no decreases in either the asset account or in the Accumulated Depreciation account. This means that the Accumulated Depreciation account should have increased by the amount of Depreciation Expense recorded in Year Two: $179,200 balance at end of Year One + $190,400 Depreciation Expense in Year Two = $369,600. Indeed, this is the balance in Accumulated Depreciation at the end of year Two (see Exhibit O). *Accumulated Depreciation balances are consistent with recorded depreciation expense each year.*

Question 6—The cash dividend actions of the company during Years One and Two probably depended on the cash flow from operations each year. What was the amount of cash inflow (or outflow) from net income each year? What were the other sources and uses of cash each year?

Answer—It would be most convenient if companies reported cash flow statements that clearly presented the cash flow from net income as well as the other sources and uses of cash during the year. But few do. So to answer the question we'll have to prepare a cash flow statement for each year. The starting point is the cash flow analysis of operations for each year.

We'll use the same approach and format explained in Chapter 14, except that the Cash Flow Statements, like the Balance Sheets and Income Statements shown in Exhibit O, will be prepared in a two-year comparative layout.

Exhibit P on page 148 shows the company's Cash Flow Statements for each year.

EXHIBIT P—CASH FLOW STATEMENTS FOR YEARS ONE AND TWO

	Year One		Year Two	
Cash Flow from Operations				
Net Income (from Income Statement)		$ 157,400		$ 243,800
Negative Cash Flow Factors:				
Accounts Receivable Increase	$ 330,000		$ 286,000	
Inventory Increase	572,000		148,000	
Prepaid Expenses Increase	84,000	($ 986,000)		($ 434,000)
Positive Cash Flow Factors:				
Depreciation	$ 179,200		$ 190,400	
Prepaid Expenses Decrease			14,000	
Accounts Payable Increase	190,400		149,800	
Accrued Expenses Increase	64,000		18,000	
Income Tax Payable Increase	27,000	$ 460,600	20,000	$ 392,200
Cash Flow from Operations		($ 368,000)		$ 202,000
Cash from Financing				
Short-Term Borrowing	$ 160,000		$ 140,000	
Long-Term Borrowing	100,000		100,000	
Capital Stock Issue	1,200,000	$1,460,000	—0—	$ 240,000
Uses of Cash				
Cash Dividends to Stockholders	$ —0—		$ 100,000	
Purchases of Long-Lived Assets	896,000	($ 896,000)	56,000	($ 156,000)
Increase in Cash during year		$ 196,000		$ 286,000

For Year One, all the amounts in the Cash Flow Statement are taken directly from the Balance Sheet at the end of the year (see Exhibit O). Since Year One is the first year of business all the assets, liabilities, and stockholders' equity accounts started the year with zero balances. Thus their ending balances are also the amounts of increase during the year.

Not so in the second year. In Year Two the amounts in the Cash Flow Statement have to be calculated by subtracting beginning balances from ending balances. (Sometimes comparative Balance Sheets report the increase or decrease of every account during the year, but usually not.)

Question 7—Why is there a large *negative* cash flow from operations in Year One, but a fairly healthy *positive* cash flow from net income in Year Two?

Answer—The first year, being the start-up year of business, puts very heavy demands on cash. Not all the sales revenue was collected; at the end of Year One notice that Accounts Receivable was $330,000, which means that this much of the sales revenue was not converted into cash. Next, the company had to build-up a stock of inventory from scratch. At the end of Year One the company had $572,000 invested in goods (products), which is the balance of Inventory. In addition to the goods sold, the company bought another $572,000 of goods that were in Inventory at the end of Year One. Notice that the receivables' increase and the inventory increase are shown as negative cash flow factors in Year One's Cash Flow Statement (Exhibit P).

Also, the company had to prepay certain expenses in the amount of $84,000 at the end of the first year, which is in addition to the expenses reported in the Income Statement for the year. The prepaid items were not deducted against sales revenue until the second year. But these items required cash payment in Year One.

Taken together these three demands on cash add-up to $986,000: ($330,000 Accounts Receivable + $572,000 Inventory + $84,000 Prepaid Expenses = $986,000 total).

The $179,200 depreciation expense recorded in Year One did not require a cash outlay, so this amount is shown as a positive cash flow factor, as you can see in the Cash Flow Statement for Year One (Exhibit P).

The company's short-term (current) operating liabilities increased during Year One (see Exhibit P). The company was relieved of paying out cash during the year. *The final result, as you can see in the Cash Flow Statement for Year One, is the $368,000 cash outflow from net income.* This cash outflow should have been planned for at the start of the year. The relatively large outflow is undoubtedly the reason the company paid no cash dividends during the first year.

In Year Two cash flow from net income is positive, although less than net income. This is typical in moderate growth years such as the company experienced in its second year of business. The company paid $100,000 cash dividends in Year Two, which is just about half of its $202,000 cash flow from net income in the year (Exhibit P).

During Year Two the company had fairly sizable increases in its Accounts Receivable and Inventory (see Exhibit P). But Prepaid Expenses decreased a little, and with the effects of depreciation and increases in its current operating liabilities the cash flow from net income did not suffer too much.

Question 8—How would you evaluate the profit performance of the company in its first 2 years?

Answer—Notice first of all that you are *not* being asked to put a market value on the company's stock shares nor on the company as a whole—a process that starts with profit performance, but goes much, much further. Instead, you are being asked to judge the company's profit performance so far. In other words, you are being asked to make a few basic measures of how well or how poorly the company has done in earning net income.

The return on equity (ROE) ratio is the most important measure of profit performance. ROE is the baseline test of profit performance for all businesses. For each year the ROE is computed as follows for the company in this example (see Exhibit O for data):

		Year One	Year Two
Return on Equity (ROE) $= \dfrac{\text{Net Income}}{\text{Total Stockholders' Equity}} =$		$\dfrac{\$157,400}{\$1,357,400}$	$\dfrac{\$243,800}{\$1,501,200}$
		11.6%	16.2%

The 11.6% ROE in Year One is not good, except when allowing for the fact that it was the company's first year of business. In their first year or two of operations, many businesses suffer losses, so any profit can be viewed favorably in these early years. However, relative to the high interest rates these days, a ROE of around 12.0% is not good. The stockholders take much more risk than lenders and quite rightly demand a higher rate of return on their capital investment.

The second year is much better; the 16.2% ROE is above average for most businesses. The managers and stockholders of the company should compare the 16.2% ROE with the average ROE for other companies in the same line of business.

Last, keep in mind that ROE is *not* a measure of cash income received by the stockholders. In Year One no cash dividends were paid, so the stockholders earned no cash income on their capital investment in the company. The value of their shares may have increased, based on the demonstrated profit earning ability of the company. But the stockholders' cash income yield was zero.

In Year Two $100,000 cash dividends were paid, which is 6.7% of the $1,501,200 stockholders' equity at the end of Year Two. So a 6.7% cash income yield was realized by the stockholders on their investment. The other 9.5% of the ROE (16.2% ROE—6.7% cash dividend = 9.5%) was retained in the business and was not available to the stockholders. The market value of their stock shares may have increased with the improved profit performance shown in Year Two.

Question 9—Did the company take advantage of financial leverage in both years? How much did financial leverage help net income?

Answer—Financial leverage refers to using borrowed funds, presumably to good advantage. To realize a financial leverage gain the company had to earn a higher annual rate of return before income tax on its assets than the annual interest rate on its debt.

The company paid 10.0% annual interest each year (see Exhibit O for data):

$$\text{Year One: } \frac{\$26,000 \text{ Interest Expense}}{\$260,000 \text{ Total Borrowed Debt*}} = \begin{array}{l}10.0\% \text{ annual}\\ \text{interest rate}\end{array}$$

$$\text{Year Two: } \frac{\$50,000 \text{ Interest Expense}}{\$500,000 \text{ Total Borrowed Debt*}} = \begin{array}{l}10.0\% \text{ annual}\\ \text{interest rate}\end{array}$$

What was the company able to earn on these borrowed funds? For each year the rates of earnings are computed as follows (see Exhibit O for data):

			Year One	Year Two
Return on Assets Before Income Tax	=	$\dfrac{\text{Operating Earnings}}{\text{Total Assets}}$ =	$\dfrac{\$340,800}{\$1,898,800}$	$\dfrac{\$537,600}{\$2,470,400}$
			17.9%	21.8%

In both years the company's pre-tax ROA is higher than its annual interest rate. There is a favorable spread, and the company realized a financial leverage gain.

In Year One the spread is 7.9%, so the company earned 7.9% more profit before income tax on its debt than it had to pay in interest. But not very much debt, only $260,000, was used. A 7.9% gain on $260,000 is only $20,540, which is not

---

*These amounts are the sum of short-term and long-term notes payable each year. It is assumed, to simplify, that the amounts were borrowed for the entire year.

---

very significant compared to the company's $314,800 earnings before income tax for the year.

In Year Two the spread is 11.8% and the company used $500,000 debt. So the financial leverage gain before income tax is about $59,000, which again is not very large compared with the company's total earnings before income tax in Year Two.

One financial strategy for the future is to take greater advantage of financial leverage. The company could finance its growth over the next year or two by taking on additional debt.

Question 10—How would you evaluate the short-term and long-term solvency (or debt-paying ability) of the company?

Answer—Even a very quick look at the company's Balance Sheets (Exhibit O) reveals that the company has not much debt relative to its stockholders' equity, which is the permanent capital base of the business. Also a quick glance reveals that the company's current assets are easily more than twice its current liabilities.

Should we bother, therefore, to calculate the debt to equity and current ratios? Quick mental arithmetic tells us the ratios are safe. Here's an instance where it appears that it may be a waste of time to compute the solvency ratios.

However, there's more to the ratios than just testing for danger signals that point to solvency problems facing the company. Another purpose is to compare the ratios with industry-wide ratios. Also, knowing the ratios allows us to get a better feel for the slack, or extra margin of safety in the ratios, and to have some idea of the fall-back safety cushion indicated by the ratios.

So it's useful to compute the solvency ratios (see Exhibit O for data), which provide the answers to Question 10:

Solvency Ratio		Components	Year One	Year Two
Current Ratio	=	Current Assets	$1,182,000	$1,888,000
		Current Liabilities	$441,400	$769,200
			2.7 to 1.0	2.5 to 1.0
		Cash +		
Quick Ratio	=	Accounts Receivable	$526,000	$1,098,000
		Current Liabilities	$441,400	$769,200
			1.2 to 1.0	1.4 to 1.0
Debt to Equity Ratio	=	All Liabilities	$541,400	$969,200
		Total Stockholders' Equity	$1,357,400	$1,501,200
			.40 to 1.0	.65 to 1.0

Question 11—Sales revenue increased 33⅓% in Year Two: Was the company able to maintain the same average credit terms and collection experience in Year Two as in Year One? If there were changes, what was the cash flow impact?

Answer—First, let's check to see that total sales revenue in Year Two increased 33⅓% over Year One:

$$\frac{\$4,576,000 \text{ sales revenue year two}}{\$3,432,000 \text{ sales revenue year one}} = \text{133⅓\%, or a 33⅓\% increase}$$

Thus if credit terms and collection experience remained the same, Accounts Receivable should have increased 33⅓%. A 33⅓% increase in Accounts Receivable would give a balance at the end of Year Two of $440,000: ($330,000 × 133⅓% = $440,000). However, as you can see in the Balance Sheet (Exhibit O), Accounts Receivable is $616,000 at the end of Year Two—much more than what it "should be."

At the end of Year One the company had 5 weeks of sales in Accounts Receivable, computed as follows:

Year One

$$\frac{\$3,432,000 \text{ Sales Revenue}}{\$330,000 \text{ Accounts Receivable}} = \text{10.4 Accounts Receivable Turnover Ratio}$$

$$\frac{52 \text{ weeks}}{10.4 \text{ Accounts Receivable Turnover Ratio}} = 5 \text{ weeks}$$

However, at the end of Year Two the company had 7 weeks of sales in Accounts Receivable, computed as follows:

Year Two

$$\frac{\$4,576,000 \text{ Sales Revenue}}{\$616,000 \text{ Accounts Receivable}} = \text{7.43 Accounts Receivable Turnover Ratio}$$

$$\frac{52 \text{ weeks}}{7.43 \text{ Accounts Receivable Turnover Ratio}} = 7 \text{ weeks}$$

The company's receivables show a somewhat alarming increase from 5 to 7 weeks during Year Two. This may be the result of easing credit terms to attract additional customers, or it could indicate that collections from customers got out of control.

In any case, the impact on cash flow is substantial. *Relative to the 5 weeks benchmark of Year One Accounts Receivable are $176,000 too high at the end of Year Two: ($616,000 actual − $440,000 "ought to be" = $176,000 excess). This means that cash receipts from customers during Year Two were $176,000 short. Thus cash flow from operations in Year Two was penalized $176,000.*

Put another way, if the shift from 5 weeks to 7 weeks average customer credit policy was a deliberate change in company policy, the managers should have clearly understood that cash flow from net income in Year Two would be $176,000 less than if the policy had not been changed.

Question 12—Did the company's inventory holding period change in Year Two? If so, what was the impact on cash flow?

Answer—A business needs to have inventory on hand when it's needed to make sales, of course. But at the same time a business should avoid holding inventory too long before it's needed. The average inventory holding period each year is computed as follows:

Year One

$$\frac{\$2,288,000 \text{ Cost of Goods Sold}}{\$572,000 \text{ Inventory}} = \frac{4.0 \text{ Inventory}}{\text{Turnover Ratio}}$$

$$\frac{52 \text{ weeks}}{4.0 \text{ Inventory Turnover Ratio}} = 13 \text{ weeks}$$

Year Two

$$\frac{\$3,120,000 \text{ Cost of Goods Sold}}{\$720,000 \text{ Inventory}} = \frac{4.33 \text{ Inventory}}{\text{Turnover Ratio}}$$

$$\frac{52 \text{ weeks}}{4.33 \text{ Inventory Turnover Ratio}} = 12 \text{ weeks}$$

The company managed to decrease its average inventory holding period by one week in Year Two, which helped cash flow by $60,000 in Year Two (one week's average cost of goods sold). In other words, cash flow from net income in Year Two would have been $60,000 less if the company had kept its inventory at 13 weeks instead of decreasing it to 12 weeks.

Question 13—What is the depreciation policy of the company? Is it using accelerated (ACRS) depreciation? Or, is it using longer and more realistic useful life estimates over which to depreciate its long-lived assets?

Answer—Let's divide each year's depreciation expense by the original cost of the assets being depreciated:

Depreciation Expense	$179,200	$190,400
Original Cost of Assets	$896,000	$952,000
=	1/5	1/5

Thus, the company is depreciating these assets over 5 years, which is the useful life (recovery period) allowed for these kinds of assets by the ACRS method. (See Chapter 22, pages 129 and 130 for review.) *In all likelihood, however, these assets will have useful lives longer than 5 years. So, the company is using accelerated depreciation.* This would be disclosed by the company in its footnotes (which are not given in this example).

Although companies must disclose whether they are using accelerated depreciation, they are not required to disclose what the more realistic useful life estimates of their assets are. Thus, we will assume here that the Machinery, Equipment, Furniture, and Fixtures owned by this company have a 12-year useful life estimate. Hence, the difference in the depreciation expense for each year by the two methods can be computed as follows:

Comparison of Depreciation Methods

	Year One	Year Two
Accelerated Method (see Income Statement, Exhibit O)	$179,200	$190,400
Straight-line (assuming 12-year life)	74,667	79,333
Difference in Earnings Before Income Tax	$104,533	$111,067

The choice of depreciation method makes quite a difference each year!

What is the correct or "actual" net income for each year? There's no conclusive answer to this question. Managers and other financial statement users have to keep alert to the impact on net income resulting from the choice of depreciation methods. In the last analysis, net income depends not only on the success of the company in making sales and controlling expenses, but also on which accounting methods are selected to measure depreciation and certain other expenses (as well as sales revenue in certain cases).

You have to take the numbers reported in the Income Statement with a grain of salt—the salt being that more than one accounting method is acceptable for measuring annual depreciation expense, as well as the annual cost of goods sold expense. Which leads to the next question.

Question 14—In the footnotes to its financial statements (which are not given in this chapter) the company discloses that it is using the FIFO, or first-in, first-out method to determine Cost of Goods Sold Expense and the cost value of its Inventory. So, is reported net income high or low?

Answer—The first inventory costs in are the first costs to be charged out to cost of goods sold expense; ending Inventory is reported at the most recent costs of acquisition in the Balance Sheet. This is the gist of the FIFO method.

FIFO, in periods of inflation, gives the highest gross profit and the highest asset value numbers. So net income is on the "high side."

A company could volunteer information concerning the differences that the LIFO method would have made in its reported earnings and inventory value. But few do. Businesses are unwilling to divulge how much different operating earnings would have been by using the opposite inventory method. The accounting profession has decided that external users of financial reports don't need to know this information. I disagree. Everyone concerned—managers, creditors, and stock investors—should have this information readily available, in my opinion.

Question 15—Did the company need to increase its short-term and long-term debt? Why or why not?

Answer—During Year Two the company increased its short-term debt $140,000 and increased its long-term debt $100,000 (see the two Notes Payable in the Balance Sheets in Exhibit O). Of course these cash sources are included in the Cash Flow Statement that we prepared earlier (Exhibit P on page 148).

Without the increases of short-term and long-term borrowings, the company's Cash balance at the end of Year Two would have been only $242,000 ($482,000 actual balance − $240,000 increase in total debt = $242,000). This lower Cash balance would have been equal to only 3 weeks of annual sales revenue. Some companies carry cash balances this low, but the majority prefer higher balances.

The company's actual $482,000 Cash balance at the end of Year Two is more than 5 weeks of its annual sales revenue. This may be a little high, although perhaps the company is preparing for major new asset purchases at the start of Year Three or, more generally, gearing-up for a large increase in sales and expense activity next year.

Question 16—In comparing Year Two's Income Statement with Year One's, what are the key changes? What are the major differences between the two years, in brief summary?

Answer—First, *total sales revenue increased by 33⅓%, as discussed earlier in Question 11.* Usually two factors are at work: prices and volume. Sales revenue increases, in most cases, are caused by a combination of higher sales prices and higher quantities sold. Managers should always insist that these two quite different factors be separated in the internal accounting reports to them.

Each has to be planned for and controlled in significantly different ways.

In most external financial reports, however, it is not possible to tell which factor—sales price inflation or volume increases—had the most impact. In any event, the combined effect in this case is that sales revenue increased 33⅓% over the previous year.

Managers are under constant pressure to maintain their gross profit margins—that is, to keep gross profit at an adequate percent of sales revenue. Even a small slippage in the gross profit ratio has a large impact on bottom-line net income.

In Year One the company's gross profit ratio was 33⅓% of sales revenue ($1,144,000 gross profit ÷ $3,432,000 sales revenue = 33⅓%). But in Year Two the gross profit ratio slipped to 31.8%. This decline is more serious than it may appear. The drop is 1.5 percentage points on sales revenue (33.33% − 31.80% = about 1.5 percentage points), which may not look that bad. But earnings before tax in Year Two is only about 11.7% of sales revenue. The fall-off of 1.5% relative to 11.7% pre-tax profit is indeed quite a big bite out of the company's profitability.

Operating Expenses increased only about 17% in Year Two, ($728,000 in Year Two ÷ $642,000 in Year One = 116.67%). This is somewhat unusual given the sales revenue increase of 33⅓%. The company's managers certainly should have examined the individual expenses making up this item in the Income Statement, to see which particular expenses were slow to increase and to determine whether this is a one-time effect or whether it will be a continuing pattern of behavior in future years.

Creditors and outside investors reading financial statements do not have access to such inside information. These users can make note of such changes but are hard pressed to know the reasons why. Generally speaking, over the long-term operating expenses tend to rise at more or less the same rate as sales revenue and costs of goods sold, although year to year there may be exceptions.

Depreciation expense has already been discussed (Question 13). *Interest expense increased because of the increases in short-term and long-term notes payable.*

Income tax expense, because the rate in both years is 50%, increased in exact proportion to the increase in earnings before tax. Congress changes the basic federal income tax rates occasionally and every year makes changes in various provisions in the federal income tax law, all of which make it very difficult to adopt any simple rule of thumb as to what the federal income tax should be as a percent of earnings before tax. (Also, most states tax business profits earned in their boundaries.)

Net income increased about 55% in Year Two ($243,800 ÷ $157,400 = 154.9%). However, this does not mean net income will increase 55% again in Year Three. The gross profit ratio may continue to slide, operating expenses may start to increase in proportion to sales revenue increases, the depreciation expense may take a big jump next year—all these may push down on net income even if sales revenue increases again next year. The growth of sales revenue may slow down next year or even decrease, for that matter.

Of course the future is uncertain. But the type of comparative analysis we have just made provides the essential starting point for assessing the prospects of any business, based on its past performance. Good luck!

INDEX